Turnaround Principals

Turnaround Principals

Passionate Leaders Who Can Improve Low-Performing Schools

Kishia C. James

ROWMAN & LITTLEFIELD
Lanham • Boulder • New York • London

Published by Rowman & Littlefield
An imprint of The Rowman & Littlefield Publishing Group, Inc.
4501 Forbes Boulevard, Suite 200, Lanham, Maryland 20706
www.rowman.com

86-90 Paul Street, London EC2A 4NE, United Kingdom

Copyright © 2022 by Kishia C. James

All rights reserved. No part of this book may be reproduced in any form or by any electronic or mechanical means, including information storage and retrieval systems, without written permission from the publisher, except by a reviewer who may quote passages in a review.

British Library Cataloguing in Publication Information Available

Library of Congress Cataloging-in-Publication Data

Names: James, Kishia C., 1977– author.
Title: Turnaround principals : passionate leaders who can improve low-performing schools / Kishia C. James.
Description: Lanham : Rowman & Littlefield, [2021] | Includes bibliographical references and index. | Summary: "The book will offer a progressive perspective of turnaround principals and enhance the current turnaround school literature"— Provided by publisher.
Identifiers: LCCN 2021033681 (print) | LCCN 2021033682 (ebook) |
  ISBN 9781475860429 (Cloth) | ISBN 9781475860436 (Paperback) | ISBN 9781475860443 (ePub)
Subjects: LCSH: School improvement programs—United States. | School principals—United States.
Classification: LCC LB2822.82 .J29 2021 (print) | LCC LB2822.82 (ebook) | DDC 371.2/012—dc23
LC record available at https://lccn.loc.gov/2021033681
LC ebook record available at https://lccn.loc.gov/2021033682

To my late and beloved father, Benjamin E. Carrington, Sr., and my beloved mother, Jacqueline R. Carrington, your unconditional love and support will never be forgotten. Thank you for never giving up on a child that was once lost but now found.

Contents

List of Figures — ix

List of Tables — xi

Foreword — xiii

Preface — xv

Acknowledgments — xvii

Introduction — xix

1 Understanding the Concept of School Turnaround — 1

2 The Fallout from Turnaround Efforts — 9

3 The Philosophical Underpinnings of Critically Conscious Leaders — 21

4 The Critically Conscious Principal in Action — 37

5 Lessons Learned from Critically Conscious Leaders — 55

6 Conclusion — 77

References — 83

Index — 97

List of Figures

Figure 2.1 Federal Portion of School Funding   13
Figure 2.2 School Funding in 2008 and 2014   14
Figure 3.1 Adverse Factors in a Turnaround School That a
            Critically Conscious Principal Will Address   26

List of Tables

Table 5.1	Participant Demographics	58
Table 5.2	Themes from In-Depth and Semi-structured Interviews	59

Foreword

There are countless books on school transformation, but not like Dr. Kishia James's *Turnaround Principals: Passionate Leaders Who Can Improve Low-Performing Schools*. Overall, this book pays equal and integrative attention to the moral responsibility of improving low-performing schools—specifically those attended by African American and Latino students—and the specific skills critically conscious leaders employed to successfully transform their schools. It will cause you to rethink turnaround leadership in ways that you have not thought about.

The nature of turnaround leadership of low-performing schools these days is badly outdated, as evidenced by the long-standing failure to make improvements. We need leadership that connects the passions of progressive principals in turnaround schools, with the lived experiences of successful leaders and the exemplary skills and practices that garnered success for their schools. *Turnaround Principals* lays out how understanding federal funding and policies of turnaround schools, combined with social justice leadership, can shift the educational landscape for many students enrolled in American K-12 public schools.

Every chapter has gems of insight. The easy-to-read format alone gives the reader clear and compelling research on why transformational, yet compassionate, leadership is a matter of equity. Chapter 1 provides a historical perspective of the turnaround concept. Moreover, it examines the social and economic factors that have contributed to school turnaround. Chapter 2 explores the federal policies and government funding which oftentimes serve as the impetus for failing schools. The exemplars of successful principals are discussed in Chapter 3, followed by Chapter's 4 discussion of the challenge leaders face when working to effect change within the school community. The passions and trials of transformational leaders—who lead with a social justice lens—are the focus of chapter 5. The book concludes with chapter 6, explaining why empowering students and teachers are requisites to shift the current educational landscape.

All of Dr. James's chapters are based on her own research and professional experiences as a turnaround leader in two schools. The book reveals miscalculations and lessons learned by various leaders and takeaways for aspiring turnaround principals. *Turnaround Principals* connects us to practical work. What makes this book so timely is that school districts are now stuck—more than ever—after the Covid-19 pandemic and continue to be mired in the status quo. Dr. Kishia James offers a way forward.

Tawannah Allen
Associate Professor
High Point University

Preface

It has been a little over twenty-five years since graduating from an all-Black inner-city high school in Durham, North Carolina. Not knowing then, but now realizing that my own high school would have been considered a turnaround school had the federal government termed persistently low-performing schools as such, in the mid-1990s. My educational and career experiences prepared me to embrace an unwavering disposition to support struggling students in some of the toughest, most depressing turnaround high and elementary schools.

As I matriculated from high school and entered the beginning phase of my career, I questioned why some schools received the latest version of a textbook or better quality textbooks, while other schools were being allowed to persistently fail or shut down to only send already struggling students to other failing schools. Eventually, my thirst drove me to lead and facilitate change for the most marginalized and vulnerable students in district offices with an eagle's view of the problems.

As I attempted to tackle the problems of the education system, I quickly realized the extra ammunition some educational leaders hold for people like myself. It took no time to comprehend other educational leaders' underlying agenda to hide wrongdoings, hire Black tokens to maintain the status quo, and continue to not provide all students with the civil right of an equitable education.

Furthermore, those like myself, in opposition to the political and racist agendas, were silenced or Blackballed from being promoted to higher positions. Nevertheless, my resilience has taken root. Helping other educational leaders in their social justice efforts and continuing to support students and families during their worst adversities will remain my mission. Regardless of others' treachery, my life's purpose will not be silenced.

The writing of this book came about because even though I can be fairly shy at times and still get anxious when speaking in public, a spark of fire comes about when others are discriminated against or mistreated based on the color of their skin. My educational and career experiences have been complex, to say the least, because teachers' and school counselors showed favoritism to those who were outspoken or in higher level classes, but what about the diamonds in the rough?

I wrote this book to explain the importance of educational leaders, teachers, school counselors, social workers, and so on, to take notice of the "diamonds in the rough." My hope is for people to become critically conscious of the systems and structures of the educational system that have been designed for some students to not succeed. I wrote this book to shed light upon the school turnaround epidemic that so many fail to openly discuss because it's not their child's school because they were able to utilize school choice or relocate into a neighborhood with great school ratings.

It's critical to build relationships with diamonds in the rough and advocate for all students' lives like it was your own child. Writings about the historical perspectives and experiences of turnaround schools and the leaders who tirelessly attempt to transform these schools need the spotlight. For decades, the spotlight has been scarce and, even worst, the highlights of how leaders transformed and sustained a turnaround school are even more limited.

We all have the same blood through our veins, but different adverse childhood and life experiences can transition a person down a path to success or a path to destruction depending on an educator's will to go above and beyond the demands of the job. Supporting all students' matriculation not just certain students based on biases is unacceptable, and it's the role of the principal who must be conscious of the systems and structures that many have been trained to sustain.

Acknowledgments

First and foremost, I thank my Heavenly Father for His continuous grace and mercy that carried me through writing my first book. I'm nothing without His presence and shield of protection for my life.

A very special thanks to Dr. Abul A. Pitre, who always supports and encourages me to reach beyond my potential. Thank you for "cracking the door" so I may walk in because you believed in me from the beginning. Thank you for sharing your incredible knowledge, drive, and agency to see others succeed.

To Vernon, thank you for your unconditional love and support. Now, we can play golf together because I'm free.

Thank you, Dr. Lynn Weber and Dr. Deborah Justice for your editing expertise, professionalism, and spirit of joy during stressful times. The virtual smiles and laughter were appreciated more than you know.

Thank you, Dr. Tawannah Allen for coming to my rescue. The support and wisdom shared in a short period of time has not been overlooked.

Thank you, Dr. Tom Koerner for recognizing the need for this literature and giving me the opportunity to share on this platform.

Finally, to all those who have been a part of me getting to this point in my life and career: Althia Scriven, Juaneza Daniels Amos, Valeria Peacock, Donna Parker, Jim Key, Jackie Ellis, Dr. Eunice Sanders, Theresa McGowan, Michelle Hedgepeth-Smith, Samantha Carter, Justin Simmons, Beverly Logan, Erlene Lyde, Florine Moore, Brenda Fearnot, Laura Inscoe, Dr. Heidi Hill, and Michael Suitte. Thank you for the love, support, friendship, and impact you've made on my life.

Writing a book is harder than I imagined, but I'm eternally grateful for this experience and opportunity. It took an immense amount of work and it would not exist without the invaluable contributions of a number of incredible and supportive people who helped shape my life and my career.

Introduction

Every student in the United States deserves a quality education. Parents understand the significance of their child receiving a quality education because families have relocated into "good" school neighborhoods for decades. Unfortunately, families relocating into neighborhoods based on the schools' ratings have perpetuated racial and economic segregation of communities. Moreover, relocating to "good" school zones is not an option for families with a lower socioeconomic status; therefore, creating great equitable schools must become a priority and nonnegotiable when preparing the future of America.

This moral responsibility of improving low-performing schools means providing quality public education to all students, and fixing failing schools is essential (Backstrom 2019). School failure may be defined in different terms, but more than likely, "turnaround schools" is the preferred term throughout critical dialogues that attempt to fathom the complexities of school turnaround.

Decades of external forces, for example, federal policies and grants, philanthropists, nonprofit organizations, have attempted to remedy the disproportionate educational outcomes of students with little success. Yet, many people have limited to no knowledge of school turnaround if their child attends a high performing school or if being employed in a low-performing school has never been a career experience.

Currently, the pandemic has illuminated educators' tireless efforts to educate the future leaders of society. Student learning has shifted to the forefront of school turnaround priorities since impoverished communities are engulfed with violence, substance and alcohol abuse, food and shelter insecurities, limited healthcare and mental health resources, and so on. Consequently, African American and Latino students are historically born into systems of inequities in healthcare, housing, education, and criminal justice that systematically threaten students' opportunities, well-being, and lives (Seider and Graves 2020).

Unfortunately, these inequities harvest adverse childhood experiences which create life-long emotional, mental, and health problems for vulnerable students. During President Barack Obama's 2010 State of the Union Address, he declared the launch of "a national competition to improve schools . . . and turn around failing schools that steal the future of too many young Americans, from rural communities to the inner city" (Obama 2010).

An understanding of America's institution of systemic racism sheds light on the existence of turnaround schools, but more importantly, being cognizant of how turnaround schools' leaders transform a school is critical when attempting to overhaul the widespread problem. Nevertheless, a true understanding of the origins of school turnaround starts with a historical perspective. The existence of turnaround schools in one of the wealthiest countries in the world is troubling.

A critically conscious pioneer, Paulo Freire ([1970] 2000) believed that "to surmount the situation of oppression, people must first critically recognize its causes, so that through transforming action they can create a new situation, one which makes possible the pursuit of a fuller humanity" (47). President Barack Obama believed that "a child's course in life should not be determined by the zip code" (Slack and Oken 2014).

Yet, patterns of residential segregation exist, and thus segregation of schools has been a long-standing issue that severely impacts the education of millions of students. Historically, the Federal Housing Administration (FHA), a United States government agency created racialized lending policies known as redlining that made it all but impossible for African Americans to access mortgages that were readily extended to Whites (Underhill, Brunsma, and Byrd 2019). African Americans were more likely to live in "D-rated" neighborhoods, which were considered "hazardous" (Badger 2017).

Although redlining occurred eighty years ago, the economic inequality still remains nationally. Furthermore, two-thirds of neighborhoods deemed "hazardous" are still populated with a majority of African American and Latino residents (Jan 2018). In association with school turnaround, communities that endured the effects of redlining have chronically failing schools based on a multitude of structural and systemic factors that includes White flight and economic collapse. The social and economic shortcomings for many African American and Latino students can be directly interrelated with the enrollment status of a turnaround school.

As a result, school turnaround has become a billion-dollar business that spotlights a subset of unique chronically failing schools with persistent challenges, struggles, and limited sustainable improvement. The U.S. Department of Education Institute of Education Services recognized the severity of America's failing schools and coined turnaround schools as a (1) chronically poor-performing school with a high proportion of students failing to meet state standards of mathematics and reading proficiency over two or more consecutive years and (2) showing substantial gains in achievement in a short time (Herman, Dawson, Dee, Greene, Maynard, Redding, and Darwin 2008).

More importantly, African American and Latino children represent the greatest number of student enrollments in high-poverty elementary and secondary public schools (Aladjem, Birman, Orland, Harr-Robins, Heredia, Parrish, and Ruffini 2010). Also, 45 percent of African American students attended high-poverty schools compared to 8 percent of White students in 2015 and 2016 (Aladjem, von Glatz, Hildreth, and McKithen 2018).

Kutash, Nico, Gorin, Rahmatullah, and Tallant (2010) revealed that 2.5 million students, particularly high-poverty students and students of color, were at risk of or already receiving a woefully inadequate education. Hence, the critical consciousness of turnaround principal alters the educational experiences of marginalized students. Although turnaround schools are known for inadequate pedagogy, the root cause to the catastrophes can be traced to unsuccessful leadership and unsustainable improvements to the school culture and climate.

Literature surrounding turnaround schools have generally revealed scarce findings of successful turnaround leaders. For this, the school leader who takes the realm of turnaround schools cannot be less than exceptional. Over forty years of evidence suggests that effective school leaders drastically influence student achievement and aspects of school performance (Public Impact 2016). Thus, a critically conscious turnaround leader recognizes and challenges stagnant school cultures and climates, along with striving to change students' educational experiences.

In order to address the long-lasting failures of turnaround schools, the stories of the lived experiences of successful turnaround principals must be highlighted. By acknowledging the narratives of successful turnaround principals, one might capture the immense challenges and barriers that contribute to high turnover rates of turnaround principals. Whether the turnover rates are based on toxic stress, upper administration dismissal schemes, or lack of consciousness to meet the needs of the school community, one thing remains the same—successful turnaround principals are rare due to external and internal affairs of a turnaround school.

Nationally, one in five schools loses its principal each year. The average climbs to one in three for low-performing schools (Harbatkin and Henry 2019). For turnaround schools, principals remain in the role less than three and half years. Thus the change of school leadership or principal mobility disrupts any possible sustainable school improvement efforts and impacts student achievement. Based on turnaround principals' brief tenure, improving the life outcomes of marginalized students is once again at risk due to transient educational leaders.

Nevertheless, there is hope by way of universities and colleges becoming analytical when preparing pre-service and in-service educational leaders. Through a critical pedagogical leadership lens, turnaround principals develop a critical consciousness to support teaching and learning. Critical consciousness, as described by Freire, requires individuals to gain knowledge of the systems and structures that create and sustain inequity (critical analysis), develop a sense of power or capability (sense of agency), and commit to act against oppressive conditions (El-Amin, Seider, Graves, Tamerat, Clark, Soutter, Johannsen, and Malhotra 2017).

As an originator of the consciousness for African Americans, Carter G. Woodson believed that African Americans were never truly educated, primarily because the program for uplifting African Americans had to be based on a scientific study of African Americans where they could empower themselves which their oppressor would never do (Woodson [1933] 2018, 66). While Woodson's beliefs were based on the existence of African Americans well over eighty years ago, the issue with America's educational system continues to present problems that must be addressed.

Thus, the critically conscious turnaround principal is unique in the educational landscape. Many educational leaders are appointed or placed by the upper administration based on persistent school failure as well as the urgency to restructure from state educational departments. The critically conscious turnaround principal commits to student learning with a critical lens to gradually recover student achievement and dismantle oppressive school cultures and climates.

The critically conscious leader is not neutral but rather a leader of activism and a leader of transformative political work (Dillard 1995, 560). Literature continues to highlight turnaround principals as the linchpin of success, and it plays a critical role in developing the capacity of systemic and shared leadership throughout the school, which is the catalyst for a healthy, safe, and supportive learning environment (Parrett and Budge 2012).

In addition, strong school leaders are identified as powerful, empowering, and transformative, with a steady commitment to bold change in the face of political and bureaucratic establishments that typically favor the status quo (Backstrom 2019). Some literature reports convey turnaround principals' different competencies; however, critical consciousness of an exceptional principal is the ability to recognize inequities and commit to change with a revolutionary intelligence that scrutinizes unjust school communities.

Therefore, critically conscious individuals understand the historical, political, economic, and social role of education in maintaining oppressive structures (Pitre 2015). This consciousness of some turnaround principals addresses and eradicates racial and social justice issues unapologetically because students' educational experiences are a priority. Withstanding a Trump era, the sense of urgency must concentrate on altering the educational outcomes of marginalized and vulnerable students.

Educational leaders have an array of challenges, which they should acknowledge, based on the multitude of struggles that students withstand, that is, chronic mental health, disproportionate suspensions and expulsions, suicidal ideation, homelessness, food insecurity, and so on. Thus, purposeful selection of critically conscious turnaround principals can address equity issues and revolutionize the academic outcomes of millions of students. Critically conscious turnaround principals' sense of agency creates an endless possibility to alter America's global and economic outlook.

OUTLINE OF THE BOOK

The book draws from critical educational theoretical frameworks that shed light on systemic inequities that pervade educational systems. *Turnaround Principals: Passionate Leaders Who Can Improve Low-Performing Schools* includes chapters that present the historical perspective of turnaround schools, an analysis of grassroot efforts of turnaround schools, federal policy influences, and narratives of successful critically conscious principals who transformed a turnaround school.

The chapters include the current literature of turnaround principals and successful turnaround principals' sustainable efforts. Additionally, the chapters are designed to support pre-service and in-service educators, scholars, and practitioners with an understanding of how turnaround schools may be transformed with a particular type of leader. The book is divided into six chapters.

Chapter 1 presents the origins of school turnaround. This chapter reveals how redlining of communities, eighty years ago, still impacts turnaround schools. The few sustainable efforts of turnaround schools link the importance of the historical perspective. The chapter goes beyond mere reporting turnaround schools' outcomes and the competencies of an educational leader; it examines historical, social, and economic factors that have contributed to school turnaround.

Chapter 2 continues with a presentation of the influences of federal policies, nonprofit organizations, and philanthropists. This chapter communicates the persistent efforts of the federal government, funding billions of dollars to state departments to improve chronically failing turnaround schools. Yet school turnaround remains a topic of discussion among many in the educational landscape.

Following the discussion of the conception of school turnaround and the influences of federal policy, chapter 3 offers the basis of a critically conscious leader and conveys the need for progressive principals in turnaround schools. The chapter highlights the work of distinguished scholars who were strong advocates and critically conscious about the need to transform education and schools. Critically conscious principals exemplify specific skills that alter schools and this chapter outlines the uniqueness of these individuals.

Chapter 4 focuses on the current research with regard to the experiences of turnaround principals. The lived experience of a turnaround principal can be unique with a number of challenges when attempting to change the school community. This chapter reveals the trials and tribulations of turnaround principals. The reader will gain a better understanding of the "sink or swim" mantra. Based on the federal government's definition of turnaround schools, principals have to drastically transform the school in two years which contributes to the "sink or swim" mantra.

Chapter 5 addresses one of the most important aspects of the book, the lessons learned from critically conscious turnaround principals. The stories of the lived experiences from critically conscious turnaround principals help readers understand the internal struggles of a turnaround school while also sharing the rewarding aspects of being a turnaround principal. This chapter includes unique themes from turnaround principals' lived experiences that are associated with a passion to be a transformative social justice leader.

Chapter 6 focuses on the importance of hiring critically conscious turnaround principals. Historically, turnaround schools have been chronically failing for three or more consecutive years. Yet, with a leader who is strategically appointed to lead turnaround schools for a minimum amount of years, the epidemic of turnaround schools could notice a paradigm shift in school transformation around the country. This chapter sheds light on the significance of critically conscious leaders' autonomy. The paradigm shift will refocus the devotion of turnaround leaders and improve student outcomes.

The final chapter provides a promising outlook of improved educational experiences for millions of marginalized and vulnerable students. Critically conscious leaders have the ability to change the world with critical pedagogy. Turnaround leaders have the ability to empower and liberate students and teachers who will shift the educational landscape. Moreover, researchers, scholars, and school districts must be willing to engage in-service and pre-service teachers and principals to start critical dialogues that recognize the primary factors that contribute to turnaround schools' success.

CONCLUSION

The turnaround principal leads with an unwavering approach to transform a school into a featured success story. The issues of school turnaround are not elusive but relentless. As a society, preparation of socially just, transformative, and critically conscious leaders who are equipped to make a difference in turnaround schools is desperately needed. These critically conscious leaders have to be prepared for the challenges and struggles of dismantling a culture of oppression in turnaround schools. Consequently, the plea for critically conscious principals to take the leadership realm in turnaround schools is essential for marginalized students to be afforded an opportunity of the American Dream.

Chapter 1

Understanding the Concept of School Turnaround

In the United States, low-performing schools have been a perennial problem. Although the United States is one of the most affluent countries in the world, it continues to struggle to improve academic outcomes for millions of students. Multiple attempts to improve low-performing schools—a process known as *school turnaround*—have been made, but many people are unaware of the complexity of turning around a chronically failing school. The scholarly literature remains scarce because successful outcomes are rare.

School turnaround is not, however, a lost cause. What has been missing from previous attempts is a historical analysis of the causes of chronically failing schools—particularly of the discriminatory educational landscape that has characterized schools in marginalized communities. Turnaround of these schools can emerge with sophisticated and analytical educators who recognize the racial injustices embedded in the educational system and display a critical consciousness that demands change in school communities with the greatest need.

This chapter will review some of the contributing factors to poor-performing schools and how they led to the concept of school turnaround.

THE ROOTS OF EDUCATIONAL INEQUITY

The United States has many fine schools, and students from around the globe come here to get a quality education. Unfortunately, the quality of education in our public schools varies tremendously from community to community. Schools in poor communities tend to struggle to reach educational goals. The enduring problems in high-poverty schools were summarized in the

Condition of Education 2019 report published by the National Center for Education Statistics (de Brey et al. 2019).

The report stated more than 75 percent of students in high-poverty schools are eligible for free and reduced-price lunch. African American and Hispanic students represent the largest number of student enrollments in high-poverty elementary and secondary public schools. And, some 44 percent of African American students attend high-poverty schools compared with 8 percent of white students.

An important root of school struggles in poor communities lies in, of all things, an innovative federal policy in home mortgages. In the late 1930s, a federal agency, the Home Owner's Loan Corporation (HOLC), created "residential security" maps that categorized neighborhoods according to their alleged lending risk. Neighborhoods categorized as hazardous or high risk were outlined in red on these maps.

The HOLC was a part of Roosevelt's New Deal and was tasked with buying mortgages that were close to default and extending longer mortgages to homeowners, thus preventing foreclosures. But the redlining starkly tagged neighborhoods as undesirable, causing them to miss out on capital investment that would improve the housing and economic opportunities of residents (Mitchell and Franco 2018). The redlining also perpetuated and aggravated segregation in the housing market. Eventually, it became all but impossible for African Americans in these neighborhoods to obtain mortgages that were readily extended to whites in similar circumstances (Underhill et al. 2019).

Redlining was banned by the Fair Housing Act of 1968, but its effect endures. Two-thirds of neighborhoods deemed "hazardous" are populated today with mostly African American and Latino residents (Jan 2018) and suffer from income inequality. The radical housing segregation that grew out of redlining caused an equivalent segregation of schools, and poor neighborhoods stayed poor (Petrella 2017). As a result, the education systems in these neighborhoods were underfunded and marginalized, leading to a prevalence of schools in crisis.

In addition, public school funding derives from local and state taxes, and those tax monies are distributed unevenly across the school districts. The large funding discrepancies between wealthy and impoverished schools perpetuate the effects of redlining even today (Biddle and Berliner 2002). In August 2019, U.S. lawmakers attended the Annual National Conference of State Legislators where it was shown that low-wealth districts, especially those serving concentrations of students from low-income families, were hardest hit with inequalities of cuts resulting in teacher layoffs, increased class sizes, and reduced services in areas ranging from counseling to after-school programs (Darling-Hammond 2019).

America's fragmented educational system has manifested itself in other ways as well. School systems are plagued with inadequate resources, especially in school districts with steep poverty and racial isolation (Kim et al. 2010). Students in under-resourced schools are often learning from less-experienced teachers who struggle to keep up with the demands of struggling schools. Furthermore, school buildings are normally unsafe and poorly equipped.

A 2011 U.S. Department of Education survey found that an estimated 14 million American students attended schools in need of repairs, and as much as $46 billion is needed for maintenance of schools nationally (McIntyre 2016). Two-thirds of schools were found to harbor unhealthy environmental conditions like peeling paint, crumbling plaster, nonfunctioning toilets, poor lighting, inadequate ventilation, and decrepit heating and cooling systems. And what is worse, poor school conditions impact student performance and learning (ibid.).

Also, the air quality and school building decay play an important role on the ability of students to concentrate in the classroom (ibid.). In addition, many poor schools lack the implementation of early intervention programs for struggling students or simply permit students to fall between the cracks with considerable amounts of school suspensions and mental health challenges. These persistent issues in elementary and secondary schools lead to many schools having low graduation rates once social promotion of students is no longer an option.

ATTEMPTS TO ADDRESS EDUCATIONAL INEQUITY

Given the highly segregated nature of U.S. schools and the continuing inequities of school funding, attempts to turn around struggling schools and provide educational equity across all types of communities took on greater urgency in the 1960s. A series of federal initiatives from the 1960s to the present day sought to improve school performances in poverty-stricken districts.

Elementary and Secondary Education Act (ESEA) of 1965

The Elementary and Secondary Education Act (ESEA) of 1965 was intended to provide additional resources for vulnerable students. It was part of President Lyndon Johnson's "War on Poverty." Johnson identified poverty as the "greatest barrier" to educational opportunity, recognized the role that poverty played in school outcomes (Battenfeld and Crawford 2015), and emphasized equal educational opportunities for all students.

Title I of ESEA called for improving the academic achievement of disadvantaged students and ensuring that all students have an equitable education with opportunities to obtain high-quality education. The ESEA legislation included massive grant monies for schools in need. The funding would be renewed every five years, sometimes under a new program name.

No Child Left Behind Act (NCLB) of 2001

A major revision to ESEA came during the George W. Bush administration. Concerned about America's competitiveness in the international market, the Bush administration made several important amendments and renamed the ESEA legislation as the No Child Left Behind (NCLB) Act in 2001. It represented a significant increase in the federal government's involvement with the educational outcomes of students. NCLB mandated learning standards and the heavy use of standardized testing to measure progress (Spring 2011).

The expansion of standardized testing was particularly controversial, both for its impact on instructional time and its subtle message that state and local school administrations could not be trusted to measure progress (Turner 2015; Papa and English 2011). Nevertheless, the NCLB was implemented with an immense array of initiatives that held schools responsible for the academic progress of all students (Osborne 2016).

States tested students with multiple benchmarks and end-of-the-year assessments in reading and math for elementary and middle school as well as specific end-of-course assessments for high schools. Testing results for students were reported as a whole and for subgroups, such as racial minorities, English-language learners, students in special education, and children from low-income families. The pressure to meet the official Adequate Yearly Progress (AYP) specified by NCLB was a source of stress and tension for teachers and school administrators alike.

AYP measurements infuriated many educators because it held all schools and all children on the same timeline (Turner 2015). Schools that failed to meet AYP goals for more than three years would face increased state intervention. The stress and feeling of being in the crosshairs—along with an unwelcome shift in classroom time from instruction to test preparation—caused an exodus of experienced teachers from the profession. The loss of staff and the traumatic changes to the school culture led to significant negative impacts on students' development (Battenfeld and Crawford 2015).

American Recovery and Reassessment Act (ARRA) of 2009

As NCLB was nearing expiration, the Obama administration passed several educational provisions as part of the stimulus package known as the American

Recovery and Reassessment Act (ARRA) in 2009. ARRA included three tiers of federal assistance for schools: the Race to the Top (RttT) program, the Investing in Innovation fund (i3), and school improvement grants (SIGs).

RttT awarded massive monies to only a few states with successful applications but it had a significant impact on education policy. It was primarily designed to encourage higher state standards, create new data systems, improve teacher effectiveness, increase college readiness, stimulate charter-school expansion, and strengthen low-performing schools (Howell 2015). These grants totaling nearly $4 billion were awarded in three stages in 2010. The program ended in 2015.

The i3 program was funded with $650 million in its first year. Grants were given to local education agencies and nonprofits that partnered with school districts or consortia to develop innovative practices and best practices (U.S. Department of Education 2017). The collaborative efforts of states, school districts, and communities were based on a common goal to improve student achievement and attainment—such as closing achievement gaps, decreasing dropout rates, increasing high school graduation rates, or increasing college enrollment and completion rates—through innovative practices. The i3 was succeeded in 2015 by ESSA's Education Innovation and Research program.

The SIGs were the portion of the legislation most geared toward underperforming schools. They were targeted to the lowest-performing 5 percent of public schools, which included chronically poor-performing schools with a high proportion of students failing to meet state standards for mathematics and reading proficiency over two or more consecutive years (Herman et al. 2008). Under ARRA, states and districts targeted funds at only the very worst schools—those that were in the bottom 5 percent of performance and had been low performing for an extended period of time (Hurlburt et al. 2012).

To receive the grants, schools had to choose one of four models for improvement: the turnaround model, the restart model, the transformation model, or the school closure model (Center on Innovation and Improvement 2010; David 2010; U.S. Department of Education 2009). Each of these models had specific plans, usually some combination of replacing principals, replacing teachers, adding educational supports, extending instructional hours, and so on.

These approaches were developed to encourage dramatic rather than incremental reforms (Kutash et al. 2010). Applications for SIGs began arriving in 2009. At that time, there were estimated to be more than 1,500 schools in need of turnaround across the United States (U.S. Department of Education 2015). Of these schools, some 1,399 were awarded SIGs to implement one of the four models through rigorous reforms to raise student achievement.

The most used model, with 74 percent of schools opting for it, was the transformation model, which required districts to replace the principal, increase teacher and school leader effectiveness, institute comprehensive instructional reforms, increase learning time, create community-oriented schools, and provide operational flexibility and sustained support (U.S. Department of Education 2011).

The second most used model, with 20 percent of schools opting for it, was the turnaround model, which required districts to replace the principal, rehire no more than 50 percent of the staff, and grant the principal autonomy to implement a fully comprehensive approach that should significantly improve student outcomes (Kutash et al. 2010). The least used models were the restart model, with 4 percent of schools opting for it, which reopened public schools as charter schools in which operators were typically granted substantial autonomy and held accountable for results through a contract or charter.

The school closure model, with 2 percent of schools opting for it, saw districts closing schools and enrolling students in other schools within the school district. However, students were often transferred to other low-performing schools, sometimes only marginally better performing than the original school. The years following ARRA and ESSA saw a new set of terminology come into usage, influenced by these legislative initiatives.

Although "turnaround" was the official name of one of the four models of the SIG program, during the course of the 2010s the term came to represent the comprehensive effort of the federal programs to radically improve underperforming schools (Kutash et al. 2010). In addition, "turnaround schools" came to refer to chronically poor-performing schools with a high proportion of students failing to meet state standards for mathematics and reading proficiency over two or more consecutive years (Herman et al. 2008).

TURNAROUND PARTNERSHIPS

Turnaround efforts were always intended to be collaborative, with districts assigning transformation coaches and instructional facilitators along with the collaboration and support of nonprofit and other organizations. Yet universities proved to be important partners in the turnaround process as well.

One example is Harvard University. Harvard's Graduate School of Education created a five-day specialized leadership institute for turnaround leaders to analyze and refine their school's turnaround plan and develop the skills needed for successful implementation (Harvard Graduate School of Education, n.d.). The specialized program taught individuals and school district teams how to establish high expectations for instructional quality, develop effective teams, translate data into action, and generate deep engagement among school and community stakeholders.

Additionally, the University of Virginia Partners for Leaders in Education (UVA-PLE) was formed through the collaboration of the University of Virginia's Darden School of Business and Curry School of Education to raise educational outcomes by building on the capabilities of the university's business and education programs, leading to strengthen district and school leadership (University of Virginia 2020). PLE believed that the limited effectiveness of school system leadership and K-12 organizational design was at the root of the national educational challenges and that transformational leadership would be the primary lever of any lasting K-12 system or school change.

Hundreds of universities and think tanks contributed to these efforts, but not all have been reliable partners. The U.S. Department of Education's School Turnaround Newsletter, which shared resources for states and districts, was last issued in summer 2011 (U.S. Department of Education 2016). The Center on Innovation and Improvement—an important support organization in the early years of school turnaround—ended its operation in October 2012; it had previously supported school districts by selecting an intervention model with the greatest potential to dramatically improve outcomes for students among other services (Center on Innovation and Improvement 2010).

THE EVOLUTION OF PARTNERSHIPS AND PROGRAMS

The transitory nature of school supports has often been a serious problem for turnaround efforts. And, of course, the federal programs themselves have changed names and missions as the years went by. The i3 program became the Education Innovation and Research program, and the SIG program was replaced in the Every Student Succeeds Act (ESSA) of 2015. ESSA was the law that succeeded the No Child Left Behind Act (2001), itself a reauthorization of ESEA (1965).

ESSA made major changes to federal education policy. Its grants gave states and districts much more flexibility in determining how to turn around their lowest-achieving schools. The U.S. Department of Education no longer required the use of specific school intervention models, and funds previously set aside for SIG now flowed through the regular Title I formula of fund disbursal (Klein 2019). ESSA also eliminated much of the mandated standardized testing in favor of state control over assessments and discontinued its requirement that states adopt the Common Core standards (U.S. Department of Education 2015).

For some, these were welcome changes to states and school districts that had felt overwhelmed by federal requirements and the dominance of standardized testing. Goal-setting and testing were still required, but with much broader leeway in how states would define and assess them. The legislation mandated other measures such as college counseling in all schools, regardless of income or performance. Other federal programs were adopted as well.

In 2014 the U.S. Department of Education implemented its Excellent Educators for All initiative, which called on states to develop plans that would give disadvantaged students the same access to high-quality educators as their more advantaged peers (U.S. Department of Education 2017). States were tasked with identifying gaps in access to quality teaching to low-income and minority students while also spotlighting schools that were successfully recruiting and retaining highly effective educators. Civil rights groups urged state education chiefs to ensure that schools would adequately serve historically overlooked groups of children, including English learners, students in special education, and students of color (Klein 2019).

CONCLUSION

The problem of turnaround schools has been long in developing. It has been directly impacted by decades-old policies such as redlining and racist funding structures that fund schools and communities based on local taxes. These policies have grave implications not only for education but for access to healthcare services and the accumulation of wealth within affected communities (Petrella 2017).

Since 1965, the U.S. Department of Education has spent billions of dollars on school improvement. Starting in 1965, ESEA, part of President Johnson's "War on Poverty" legislation, was innovative in acknowledging the profound effect of poverty on student performance. NCLB, passed in 2001, mandated massive standardized testing in an attempt to hold schools accountable for student progress. The programs launched in the 2009 ARRA legislation created new levels of state reporting and federal oversight, while releasing billions of dollars to states that joined the programs.

Did these turnaround efforts bear fruit? In the next chapter, we will examine the results of these decades-long attempts to help the nation's poorest-performing schools.

Chapter 2

The Fallout from Turnaround Efforts

A successful turnaround has been defined as a school that has shown substantial gains in achievement in a short time (Herman et al. 2008). But the results of turnaround efforts have been mixed, and research on successful turnaround schools is scarce. This chapter will examine the results of the intense efforts at school turnaround over the last two decades.

RESULTS OF THE TURNAROUND GRANTS

The infusion of grant money into the U.S. educational system during the Obama administration was unprecedented. In 2009, its first year of operation, as Kutash et al. (2010) report, "All told as a result of ARRA, schools received approximately $14 billion over their regular Elementary and Secondary Education Act [ESEA] appropriation. School-improvement funding received an additional $5 billion boost in 2009 due to RTTT and i3 funding."

So how did the massive infusion of money into local school districts affect schools' achievements? In 2016 the U.S. Department of Education released its "Case Studies of Schools Receiving School Improvement Grants Final Report." This study of school turnaround examined a sample of twenty-five schools that received federal SIGs in 2010–2011 and 2012–2013 and submitted their data back to the Department of Education in spring of 2011 and spring of 2012.

Of these twenty-five core schools, a subsample of twelve schools were selected to collect data in the spring of 2013 and were the focus of more in-depth analyses across all three years of their SIG funding. The report gave insight into the amount of staff rotation that the SIG schools experienced. Out of the twenty-five core sample schools, twenty-one schools replaced the principal at least once before the SIG program or in year one of the SIG program. By year two of the SIG program, nine out of the twenty-five schools replaced the principal twice.

There were only three schools within the sample that maintained the same principal over the three-year period. Of the twenty-five core sample schools, twelve schools—nine of which used the turnaround model, two the restart model, and one the transformation model—replaced at least 50 percent of their teachers during the 2009–2010, 2010–2011, and 2011–2012 school years.

In the second year of the SIG program, the principal and district officials in about three-fourths of the core sample schools believed that recruitment and retention challenges limited the school's ability to build skilled and motivated staff. On the positive side, in seventeen of twenty-one core sample schools with sufficient data, most teacher survey respondents reported learning about and changing their instructional practices after participating in professional development on mathematics, literacy, or data use. However, student gains were not evident.

Results related to the sustainability of improvements under SIG funds were unsteady. Of the twelve core subsample schools, which were followed for all three years of the SIG program, two schools appeared to have strong prospects for sustainability, six schools appeared to have mixed prospects for sustainability, and the remaining four schools appeared to have weak prospects for sustainability, based on teacher survey responses and site visit data (U.S. Department of Education 2016).

Follow-up studies have shown similar failures. The U.S. Department of Education released a report in 2017 on the effectiveness of SIG funds and found that overall, across all grades, there were no significant impacts on mathematics and reading scores, high school graduation, or college enrollment. There were no statistically significant impacts on student outcomes within student and school subgroups.

At the elementary level, there was no evidence that one model was more effective at improving student achievement than the other. In higher grades, middle and high school levels, more student achievement gains were found in mathematics for the turnaround model than the transformation model, but other factors may have played a role in the differences. A report released by the Rockefeller Institute of Government concluded that the vast majority of failed turnaround efforts showed three areas of weakness that likely affected their success.

The schools lacked (1) the flexibility needed to meet the individual challenges of each school, (2) strong and powerful transformational leaders, and (3) a steady commitment to bold changes in the face of a political and bureaucratic establishment that typically favors the status quo (Backstrom 2019). The

Institute continued by stating that school turnarounds must have certain essential action elements and design characteristics for schools to hit their marks.

Having the right staff, generating an unrelenting focus on quality instruction, assessing student performance in ways that inform instructional efforts, establishing transparent and high-performance expectations, holding all school personnel accountable, and delivering early successes are among the essential elements that transformation leaders must deliver (Backstrom 2019). Again, these elements were missing from schools that failed to flourish under turnaround directives.

The leaders of turnaround schools were not required to make the bold changes needed to quickly improve; districts did not empower transformative leaders with the authority and autonomy to take these actions; and the dramatic and ongoing changes required ultimately eroded political and public support for the turnaround efforts (Backstrom 2019). Fifty years and billions of dollars of costly turnaround programs yielded very little in the way of concrete improvements.

In response to the failed attempts from the federal government, the boldest and most attention-getting school turnaround efforts were state takeovers of persistently failing schools (Backstrom 2019). The state takeovers allowed states to step in and assume direct control of failing schools, but state takeovers failed just as often as the original turnaround programs. Very few takeovers produced stellar examples of transformation into high-achieving schools. Yet a handful of school districts did improve student outcomes for a period of time—until the transformative leader overseeing the turnaround efforts resigned.

In November of 2011, Lawrence, Massachusetts, took the unparalleled step of seizing control of the Lawrence Public School District, which was known for its fifteen years of poor academic performance and scores on state exams. The district schools were in the bottom 1 percent in the state, had a 52 percent graduation rate, and had a 25 percent dropout rate. Jeff Riley was named the district's receiver and given the necessary autonomy to make dramatic reforms. Within three years, the state takeover resulted in increased test scores with record highs; the district was placed in the top quartile of urban school districts in the state; and the district improved ELA and math proficiency as well as graduation rates.

In August of 2010, Tennessee created the Achievement School District (ASD) and in August of 2012, named Chris Barbic to lead the state takeover of the lowest-performing public schools. After just the first three years, ASD saw early results that were promising. For schools under its control, proficiency on state math assessments improved from 16.3 percent to 27 percent and science proficiency increased from 16.5 percent to 26.5 percent. Unfortunately, the reading proficiency decreased.

Yet, Barbic announced that he was stepping down as the ASD superintendent after just three years. ASD ended up having three leaders within a seven-year period, and the turnaround schools showed minimal year-to-year gains and still performed significantly below the state average (Backstrom 2019). Once again, the state takeover improved student outcomes for a short period of time based on dramatic and bold transformational leadership until leadership changed and political support was eroded. In summary, federal education policy funding has skyrocketed in the past five decades, yet educational outcomes remain the same or only minimally better (Schwalbach 2018).

Failing schools seem to be destined to fail even after decades of district-wide fix-it attempts that have wasted billions of federal dollars and taxpayer dollars. School turnarounds start strong with an initial design by new leadership but often become subject to a state legislative process that is heavily influenced by special interests and preferences for maintaining the status quo (Backstrom 2019). The Southern Education Foundation cautioned that unless serious change is made, "the trends of the last decade will be prologue for a nation not at risk, but a nation in decline" (Battenfeld and Crawford 2015, 10).

WHY TURNAROUND EFFORTS FAILED

It is clear that, despite some successes, the federal turnaround efforts largely failed to transform struggling schools in poor communities. The reasons for this are varied and complex.

Funding

Despite the huge grants given to school districts, funding can still be an issue for individual schools. Because public schools rely on local and state funding to support the operations of the school, federal funds are pursued especially in turnaround schools. Most federal funds are directly sent to states and local school districts, and each state has its own formula for how they disperse that funding (Chen 2020). Some schools may not have received as much federal funding as expected, and this varies from state to state based on state legislation, application procedures, mandates, and distribution policies.

And while federal funding seems enormous, the reality can be less impressive. For example, in 2015 federal contributions only accounted for about 8 percent of school budgets nationwide (Stephens 2018). Furthermore, a report conducted by the Center on Budget and Policy Priorities found that at least thirty-one states provided less state funding per student in the 2014 school year than in the 2008 school year (figures 2.1 and 2.2), before the recession (Leachman et al. 2016).

Most K-12 schools rely heavily on state and local funding, due to the relatively low levels of federal contributions. For some school districts, targeting at least some funds to school districts with low-income families doesn't fully equalize educational spending across wealthy and poor school districts (Leachman et al. 2016). Therefore, even grants are not enough to cover all of the needs of a school population, and implementation of grant projects can be complex. For example, if schools use federal funds to provide students with laptops, that is a good start. But if students don't have Internet access at home, the expenditure is not as helpful as it was intended to be.

Sustainability

Even when turnaround does occur, often the successes are short-lived. The turnaround initiatives are usually grant-based, and once special funding for the turnaround is withdrawn, the changes typically prove unsustainable. The U.S. Department of Education's 2016 report on SIG funds provides evidence that chronically low-performing schools can change in some respects, at least in

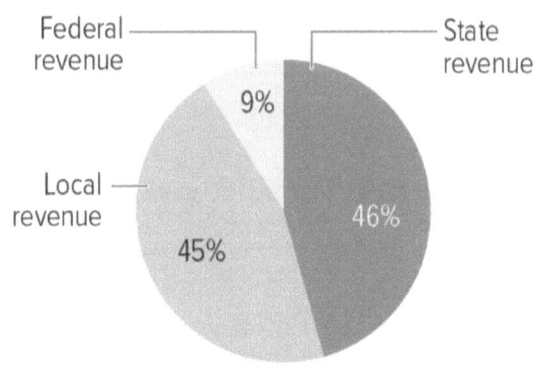

Figure 2.1 Federal Portion of School Funding.

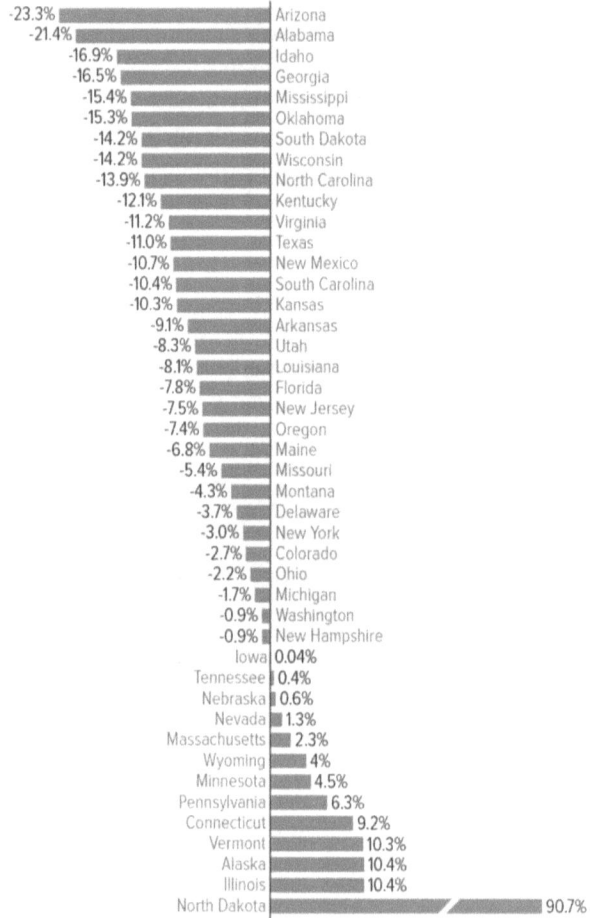

Figure 2.2 School Funding in 2008 and 2014.

the short term, with many efforts to build human capital. Yet, to sustain these changes, it appears that an equally great effort may be needed to retain any hard-won improvements—and this is difficult to do without continued funding.

Brian Backstrom with the Rockefeller Institute of Public Policy noted that many policymakers—opting to avoid rocking the boat—enact education "reforms" that, by design, provide at best only marginal and temporary improvement. But bold problems require bold solutions (Backstrom 2019).

Staffing

One important finding from the 2016 U.S. Department of Education study as well as many others is how much leadership of SIG schools matters (Papa and English 2011; Fairchild and DeMary 2011; Kutash et al. 2010; Leithwood et al. 2010; Steiner et al. [2008] 2016). Schools in which respondents described improvements were more likely to be led by principals with demonstrated elements of strategic leadership, involving a theory of action for making improvements in their school (U.S. Department of Education 2016).

Additionally, teacher survey respondents highlighted the principal's transformational leadership (principals who can motivate and engage their staff) and instructional leadership (principals who are knowledgeable about instructional issues) as reasons for improved schools. As important as strong leaders appear to be, identifying, recruiting, and retaining the most skilled principals in chronically low-performing schools is a persistent challenge (U.S. Department of Education 2016).

Mandating principal replacement in SIG schools appears to have in many cases brought stronger leaders to schools that needed a change in leadership. At the same time, a continued pattern of frequent leadership turnover in several of the case study schools undercut the schools' progress (U.S. Department of Education 2016). When school leaders depart—particularly strong, well-regarded ones that are credited with improvements—the sustainability of school improvement efforts may be threatened.

Lack of Comprehensive Change

An influx of federal funds can sometimes work as a Band-Aid approach, with the monies being used to buy supplies and hire staff but not to address more deeply rooted issues. Cultural and societal barriers create traumatic and stressful life experiences for families that ultimately affects the school performance of students. Students dealing with childhood trauma such as homelessness, racism, physical abuse, verbal abuse, sexual abuse, and emotional neglect most likely will suffer in school because the communities they live in are rife with toxicity that any child should not have to endure nor witness.

Turnaround for Children, a nonprofit organization, recognizes that children growing up in poverty face profound but predictable cognitive, social, and emotional challenges that stem directly from the effects of stress and trauma in their lives (Yu and Cantor 2016). These terrible experiences impact learning and the development of the brain. For example, a student watching a family member being abused, losing a caregiver, supporting their parent(s) or themselves by stepping into an adult role of household duties or working for the family, supporting and nurturing younger siblings, and suffering from food or housing insecurities will struggle with the enjoyment of learning because the responsibilities and emotions of adulthood have already consumed their lives.

Schools can assess how deeply their instruction is affected by these factors and learn about the Adverse Childhood Experiences (ACEs) study and how student's childhood and life experiences impact their development and learning. When schools are aware of students' challenges, then a sense of connection and empathy may take root to provide extensive supports to the student. Also, by completing the ACE Quiz, the result in scores predicts toxic stress and health complications in children if their challenges remain unaddressed.

Of course, these stresses are compounded for poverty-stricken students who attend schools with intensified stresses and dysfunctions. Many educational leaders charged with taking the helm of a turnaround school create a plan with a laser-like focus on instructional improvements, especially since many students endure external life challenges. There are endless conversations and an overwhelming number of meetings that range from discussions of pedagogical progression to reteaching foundational skills that were never mastered.

Even though instruction is normally at the top of the list of items to address, other factors include mental health challenges and social emotional needs that are often overlooked. Addressing mental health needs in school is critically important because one in five children and youth have a diagnosable emotional, behavioral, or mental health disorder and one in ten young people have a mental health challenge that is severe enough to impair how they function at home, at school, or in the community.

Focusing on improving the mental health and social emotional needs of students improves the behaviors of students. Within turnaround schools, there is normally a high rate of student suspensions, unless the principal has been warned by school district officials to strategically reduce the suspension rate of the school. It is always understood that if the behaviors of students are not maintained, then learning will not happen within the classroom setting. Therefore, addressing and implementing social emotional skills into teachers' lesson plans and throughout the school community is imperative.

Also, addressing any mental health concerns of students is necessary because if students are not mentally and emotionally prepared for learning, students, teachers, and administrators alike will develop persistent frustration with education. It is always noted that learning will never take place in the classroom setting without effective classroom management and addressing the social and emotional behaviors of students. Students must learn core content as well as behavioral skills to survive in school and society.

School turnaround does not transpire with only one major concern like instructional competency. School turnaround has a multitude of concerns that make transforming and sustaining turnaround schools extremely complex.

Traumatic Change to School Culture

Most federal education grants require drastic changes in school leadership and teaching staff. While this can sometimes be a positive change, in many cases it imposes on a school a traumatic change in school culture, causing a merry-go-round of teachers and a sense of instability in the school. This can be seen in the aftermath of the No Child Left Behind Act. When schools continuously failed to meet the criteria of the NCLB Act and missed achievement targets for more than three years, the school faced state intervention. This usually took the form of hiring a new principal and replacing a certain percentage of the teachers (Osborne 2016).

These changes caused more stress among school administrators and teachers and resulted in many great teachers leaving the teaching profession because of the complex trials and tribulations of the new school culture. In 2016, the National Center for Education Statistics (NCES) reported that 8 percent of teachers leave the profession annually, and another 8 percent move to other schools (Wang 2019). In 2017, a study by Learning Policy Institute reported that special education teachers have a 46 percent higher-than-predicted turnover rate than that of elementary teachers and that turnover rates are higher in schools with more students of color and low-income families (ibid.).

Unfortunately, the designers of NCLB failed to realize the significant negative impacts on students' development that would result from massive changes to a school culture and climate across the educational life span of a school. The focus on standardized testing, the loss of instructional time it entailed, and the punitive nature of the program drove many teachers out of the profession and proved to be a poor solution to school turnaround (Battenfeld and Crawford 2015).

These stressors were particularly hard on principals. Schools are identified as turnaround schools because they have been on the radar as chronically failing for three or more years. Many times, school district officials visit schools for observations and critiques, and then shift the leadership of the school abruptly. Observations and critiques may include more school leadership meetings to discuss the critical needs of the school, with the turnaround principal being in the spotlight.

Some examples of the type of observations or critiques may be viewed by "learning walks" to understand classroom dynamics as it relates to student engagement and pedagogy, as well as student behavior analysis within common spaces like the hallways or cafeteria. These can be insightful, and district administrators may be able to observe trends that school administrators are too close to see clearly.

Yet, some turnaround schools experience school district administrators who are domineering and demanding improvements but offering limited support. Also, some districts may hire transformation coaches to mentor turnaround principals—retired principals with a track record of improving low-performing schools or veteran educational leaders who have dedicated their careers to serving marginalized student populations. But the concentrated attention on the turnaround principal may be too great and simply add stress to an already difficult and convoluted task.

CONCLUSION

It is clear that the federal efforts on turnaround schools have been only mildly successful at best. High turnover rates of principals and teachers, lack of culturally relevant and critical pedagogy, principal and teacher burnout, limited autonomy and support from school district offices, and lack of mental health supports are all contributing factors to why many turnaround schools remain low-performing, despite the influx of money. The federal approach to school improvement has emphasized K-12 accountability over the root causes of educational inequality (Battenfeld and Crawford 2015), demanding a change in outcomes without a change in circumstances.

In addition, the requirement to reform a school in two to three years is a self-defeating standard for the administrators tasked with achieving it. Most federal programs demanded an improvement in achievement levels within a few years' time—an unlikely outcome for schools with deeply entrenched problems. Research continues to show that organizational change typically does not occur in a short period of time, and a three-to-five-year window of improvement would be more realistic than the one-to-two-year model that turnaround programs have usually demanded.

Previous findings from the school turnaround literature indicate that improvements can take up to five years to achieve (Pham et al. 2018; Aladjem et al. 2010; Berends et al. 2002; Bloom et al. 2001; Borman et al. 2003; Gross et al. 2009; Stuit 2010). Further research suggests that the effects of school turnaround can fade over time (Gill et al. 2007; Strunk et al. 2016).

For the first time, in 2013, low-income children became the majority in U.S. public schools (Suitts 2013). But we still underestimate the effect of poverty and racism on educational outcomes. Improving the areas reviewed in this chapter will help—taking a comprehensive approach to change, reducing the stress of teachers and administrators, allowing sufficient time for improvement, and so on.

We know that school turnaround—despite the dire track record of current efforts—can succeed. In the 2010s, three pioneer school districts implemented school reforms while also facing significant challenges around the issues of talent, politics, time, and money. Under the guidance of Roland Fryer Jr., the youngest African American professor to receive tenure at Harvard, his company EdLabs completed research on models of effective schooling for low-performing schools. They recommended implementing high-performing charter school practices in a traditional public school environment (Straus and Miller 2016).

Fryer and Terry Grier, former superintendent of the Houston Independent School District (HISD), worked together to dramatically confront the nine low-performing schools in the district. Fryer understood that implementing his research would require significant political will among school districts and school leaders. He and Grier worked together to launch HISD's Apollo 20 program, the nation's first large-scale effort to improve low-performing schools with school district support using charter school practices.

Based on the statistically significant improvements in math achievement in HISD, other districts such as Denver Public School District (DPS) and Lawrence Public School District in Massachusetts pursued their own customized approach to turn around low-performing schools with Fryer's guidance (Straus and Miller 2016). The success of some careful efforts has shown that school turnaround is not an impossible dream.

But to achieve more than individual, sporadic success, stakeholders must properly recognize the need for turnaround leaders with a critical consciousness. Without the presence of critical dialogues in the cultural context of American history, there will be long-term impacts that obstruct the educational experiences of students who attend turnaround schools. The challenge of finding and developing such leaders is the missing step in transforming students' academic performance.

Chapter 3

The Philosophical Underpinnings of Critically Conscious Leaders

The federal government has made efforts to improve schools affected by poverty and racism, starting with the Elementary and Secondary Education Act (ESEA) of 1965. Subsequent versions of the act, including the No Child Left Behind Act (NCLB) of 2001, the education provisions of the American Recovery and Reinvestment Act (ARRA) of 2009, and the Every Student Succeeds Act (ESSA) of 2015, continued those efforts.

The acts were generally targeted at the lowest-performing bottom 5 percent schools and required the schools to monitor progress in math and reading scores and graduation rates (Dunn and Ambroso 2019). The acts had different requirements for poor-performing schools and their school districts, but they generally tasked districts with replacing principals and staff, conducting standardized testing, and reporting results. If schools failed to make the requisite progress (sometimes within a matter of two or three years), additional actions would be taken.

Researchers have argued over the lack of reliable information regarding the results of these improvement efforts, describing the literature as "sparse" and "scarce" (Smarick 2010, 23). Despite national attention, states and school districts continue to notice a dearth of available evidence-based interventions, even in the most recent programs such as ESSA (Klein 2019). But it is clear that these turnaround efforts have been less than successful.

Most gains have been modest, and the vast majority of students in turnaround schools transition into society with deficits in skills and knowledge that all but cripple their chances at future success (Calkins et al. 2007). Turnaround for Children believed that until high-poverty schools have universal practices and supports that specifically address predictable cognitive, social, and emotional challenges that stem directly from the effects of stress and trauma of children's lives, turnaround schools will continue to underperform and millions of children will never reach their full academic and personal potential (Yu and Cantor 2016).

Furthermore, the federal government's large footprint in education has not led to sustained positive effects, in part due to its sweeping programs, which have failed to address the needs of local communities (Schwalbach 2018). Requirements for replacing staff and conducting standardized testing have been controversial, often disrupting school culture and taking valuable time away from classroom instruction.

Standardized testing skyrocketed after the NCLB Act, but many opponents of state standardized testing believed that they offered no meaningful measure of progress, have not improved student performance, and have failed to predict the future success of students; thus, standardized tests are not useful metrics for teacher evaluations (ProCon.org 2020). Furthermore, it appears that U.S. students are falling backward in terms of global competitiveness; U.S. students slipped from being ranked eighteenth in the world for math in 2000 to fortieth in 2015, from fourteenth to twenty-fifth in science, and from fifteenth to twenty-fourth in reading (ibid.).

All in all, the dispersal of federal and state funds to low-performing schools over the last fifty years has been ineffective. There is a need to reckon with this reality of low achievement and the fact that the various education interventions, strategies, policies, and regulations imposed by policymakers have failed to move the needle (Stotsky 2018). Despite how old programs have come up short, turnaround schools are not a lost cause.

If grant money, staff rehauls, and strict reporting requirements have not substantially improved struggling schools, then it is incumbent upon policymakers, universities, and education professionals to investigate why—and to develop new ideas to energize the process of school turnaround. There may be many workable ideas, but there is one key element that must be addressed for these schools to be successful. It is the nature of school leadership and the principals who guide the day-to-day operation of our public schools.

THE PRINCIPAL IN TURNAROUND SCHOOLS

The position of the principal at a turnaround school is one of the most challenging in all of American education. Turnaround principals who are successful in their efforts to improve low-performing schools are likely to be quite different from principals who have succeeded in higher-performing schools (Kowal et al. 2009). A report by Public Impact (Steiner et al. [2008] 2016) posits that turnaround principals' competencies stem from four clusters.

These include the principal (1) having a strong desire to achieve outstanding results and task-oriented actions for success, which includes a relentless focus on learning results, (2) motivating and influencing others in their thinking and behavior to obtain the desired results, (3) solving and simplifying complex problems, which includes analyzing data to inform decisions, creating clear and logical plans for staff, and ensuring a strong connection between school learning goals and classroom activity, and (4) demonstrating a public display of self-confidence by being visible throughout the school, committed, and self-assured despite the bombardment of personal and professional attacks common during turning around a low-performing school.

Furthermore, turnaround leaders are collective leaders, meaning they share decision-making and led school improvement by creating structures and incentives around a common agenda for learning among all staff; they align resources with learning activities, needs, and priorities; and they build external relations that can support a school-wide learning agenda (Wallace Foundation staff 2011). The demands of the turnaround principal are great, and the need for such leaders is even greater (Harvard Graduate School of Education, n.d.).

In addition to daily operations, budgeting, supervision of staff, and transforming the school community, the turnaround principal has to contend with the challenges that students face as part of an economically disadvantaged community, often on the receiving end of racism and discriminatory behavior and attitudes. The federal requirements of the 2000s and 2010s did not make this job easier. For example, a school identified as a turnaround school in 2005–2006 may have had, over the course of four years, four different principals and an influx of new and inexperienced teachers.

With only a few years to show results under these chaotic conditions, the school may have ultimately been ordered to close its doors, leaving its students to be transferred to nearby schools that may have been struggling just as much. As some of the most burdensome requirements for federal funding have been dropped over the years, some of these situations have become more relaxed. The Trump administration lightened the load of school accountability, leaving education matters up to the states (Jacob 2017).

Yet, with more autonomy of schools from the federal government, there is potential for greater disparity with low- and high-poverty schools, as more capable, focused, and well-resourced states pull even further ahead of those with less capacity, fewer resources, and greater political dysfunction (ibid.). Depending on the school district leaders' consciousness about the persistently failing schools, it is less likely now that a principal will be dismissed, transferred to another school through demotion to transfer as a assistant principal, or encouraged to retire after working at a struggling school.

There may be marginally less standardized testing, and as the emphasis on testing and reporting declines somewhat, it may be easier to retain teachers and staff. But this easing up of federal requirements only brings principals back to their original challenge: raising math and reading proficiencies, improving graduation rates, and providing their students with the kind of high-quality education that will allow them to succeed in the world and make the most of their talents and resources.

Aladjem and colleagues (2010) found that among the subset of schools that had rapid success in turnaround efforts, the role of the principal was particularly important. But to achieve these goals, not just any principal will do. Schools need principals who have what has become known as "critical consciousness," an awareness of how poverty and racism have shaped the communities and the school culture, and how to begin to undo the effects they have had on the students.

WHAT IS CRITICAL CONSCIOUSNESS?

Successful school turnaround begins with the selection of the principal. The principal must have all of the usual competencies for school leadership: budgeting expertise, administrative talent, the ability to motivate students and staff, and other skills. But the principal of a turnaround school must have so much more. They are often entering a school that is shouldering a history of multiple disappointments, a school that has become fragile from staff turnover and low staff morale, multiple changes of leadership in an abrupt manner, high suspension and expulsion rates, high retention and low promotion rates, mental health challenges of students that have not been addressed, high dropout rates, and a feeling of hopelessness.

In this scenario, the principal must be much more than an effective administrator. He or she must have a critical consciousness—an understanding of how external factors such as poverty and racism have contributed to the challenges that students face and what can be done to help students overcome them. Turnaround principals must unpack how the vast majority of educational leaders have been trained in programs that have held a white dominant perspective towards schools and education (Pitre 2011). School leaders, especially turnaround principals, must adhere to a social critique of schools' role in perpetuating racism, inequality, and oppression, something that is unheard of for most school leaders (ibid.).

So, what is *critical consciousness*? Critical consciousness of race, in particular, involves an awareness of how the past has shaped the present and how racist attitudes still impact the education of African American students. Racial critical consciousness was first formulated by Carter G. Woodson, the great African American educator and historian. Woodson believed that the education of African American students was fatally perverted by racism.

He found that African American students were taught according to the needs of white society, not their own needs. In his seminal volume *The Mis-education of the Negro* ([1933] 2018), he argued that African American students were educated to be workers and laborers rather than thinkers and innovators, much less citizens. He posited that they would never receive a proper education when that education was in the hands of their oppressors.

Woodson believed that including Black history in their education was key, and he founded the *Journal of Negro History* and an early version of Black History Month to provide a truer picture of Black reality and achievements. Making students aware of their history, educating them to be critical thinkers, and encouraging them to break free of the structures and desires of white America were the cornerstones of Woodson's educational philosophy (Pitre 2011, 2015).

Woodson's successor in educational philosophy was Paulo Freire, a renowned Brazilian scholar who recognized that in order to overcome the situation of oppression, people must first recognize its causes. Freire argued that oppressed individuals suffer from the dominant elites' imposition of a banking model of education, in which teachers are the active participants who choose the content and deposit it in their students. Students are passive receptacles who are expected to memorize the information that is deposited in them. Students are barred from participating in their own education in any meaningful way (Rose 2017).

Instead, their consciousness is "filled" by the dominant culture, encouraging passivity and creating a fear of freedom (Freire [1970] 2000). This model of education prevents students from developing critical thinking skills and continues to promote long-standing biases within society (Rose 2017). The answer, for Freire as for Woodson, is the creation of educational leaders and institutions that allow students to understand the ideological underpinnings and strategies of white supremacy and wealth inequality.

Freire believed that most educational systems produce and reproduce oppression; therefore, he deemed it necessary for education and schooling to *undo* oppression, supporting the creation of schools, systems, and individuals that resist white supremacy and liberate Black minds (Theoharis 2009). The critical examination of the causes of their oppression would allow students to pursue transformative action that would change their situation and allow them the pursuit of a fuller humanity.

To be critically conscious is to understand the historical, political, economic, and social role of education in maintaining oppressive structures (Pitre 2015). For thinkers like Woodson and Freire, the philosophy of liberation and critical understanding was not an educational "extra" but the very foundation of education. Critically conscious leaders were not to be neutral but rather leaders of activism and of transformative political work (Dillard 1995).

THE CRITICALLY CONSCIOUS PRINCIPAL IN TURNAROUND SCHOOLS

How does critical consciousness play out in educational leadership? To really help struggling schools, principals have to understand the many contributing factors to the school's failures. Some of these factors are attitudinal, some are administrative, and some are environmental. In all three cases, the principal must demonstrate to staff and students an awareness of these factors and the belief that change is possible—and therefore that success is possible. Figure 3.1 summarizes these factors.

Attitudinal Factors

The first key for turnaround principals is considering attitudinal factors. As a starting point, they must believe that change is possible, actively reject the status quo, and be ready to try to change the mindset of teachers and district administrators to make concrete changes in how the school is run. This is easier said than done. When turning around a failing school, there

Attitudinal Factors

- Optimism
- Teacher mindset
- Awareness of racial biases

Administrative Factors

- Suspension policies
- Gifted and talented programs
- Curriculum

Environmental Factors

- Adverse childhood experiences in the community and home
- Lead paint and other environmental risks
- School-to-prison pipeline

Figure 3.1 Adverse Factors in a Turnaround School That a Critically Conscious Principal Will Address.

are numerous policy constraints that hinder and challenge turnaround efforts (Rhim and Redding 2014).

Staffing at turnaround schools is critical because ineffective evaluation systems, restrictive certification rules, and rigid seniority-based placement are hurdles to dismissing ineffective performers. Likewise, salary scales make it difficult to reward great leaders and teachers for taking on a challenge and succeeding, and rules that limit the number of students a great teacher can have make the hard task of turning around a school even harder (ibid.).

Also, turnaround schools endure policy constraints in how they utilize resources, as certain staffing models limit principals' redesign of operations and plans to use teachers and new teaching roles to give more students access to great teachers (ibid.). The principal must be committed to doggedly pursuing change despite resistance. A 2017 review of studies on turnaround principals revealed that principals need to possess an array of competencies.

Principal candidates' leadership competencies are scored by the school districts to make hiring decisions (Steiner and Barrett 2012). Some of these are skills needed by any principal, but some are particularly key for turnaround leaders (Meyers and Hambrick Hitt 2017). Even with scarce literature surrounding the turnaround principal, it is clear that the rare turnaround principal (1) embraces centralized decision-making before making informed decisions to distribute leadership; (2) expertly yields support and accountability simultaneously to catalyze change; and (3) capitalizes on quick wins to jump-start changes in school culture (Hambrick Hitt et al. 2018).

Furthermore, turnaround principals hold a belief that positive change can happen and a competitiveness and responsiveness to change that distinguishes turnaround principals from non-turnaround principals (ibid.). Dallas Hitt highlighted emotional intelligence as a key skill because the turnaround principal is responsible for shifting the mindset of teachers and setting clear expectations. According to which teachers should believe their students can learn regardless of their backgrounds and circumstances (Meyers and Hambrick Hitt 2017).

That emotional intelligence will also be key for the concrete changes and restructuring that the principal will need to persuade district administrators to support. Hilliard (1991) argued that an educator's ability for true restructuring is drawn from an appropriate vision of human potential. He believed educators should restructure to create education systems that have never existed, not because they were hard to create but because society has not believed in or implemented an educational model that recognizes every student's ability to maximize their potential.

This is a matter of vision—the unwavering belief that the process of education (and therefore the result) can be radically altered to better serve students. Another attitudinal change is reconceptualizing the source of "failure" in the school. For the past twenty years and more, federal K-12 policies have targeted the "achievement gap" between white students and minority students. However, the focus on "underachievement" by students of color tends to obscure the role of influences outside of the school (Stotsky 2018).

With a focus on achievement gaps, culturally diverse students—including African American students, Latino/a students, English language learners, and students living in poverty—are positioned as somehow deficient in the minds, practices, and designs of educators (Milner 2010). Gloria Ladson-Billings (2006) attempted to correct this bias by conceptualizing the problem as an *education debt* rather than as an achievement gap.

She argues that the historical, economic, sociopolitical, and moral decisions and policies of the U.S. education system have created this "gap"—a gap in resources for and treatment of marginalized students, both in school and outside of it (Gale de Saxe 2019). The education debt recognizes the resources that could and should have been invested into low-income students and the deficit of resources that has led to a variety of social problems that require ongoing public investment (Ladson-Billings 2006).

The concept of education debt reframes and challenges the phrasing of the long-bemoaned achievement gap, which focuses on students' failure to succeed (Gale de Saxe 2019). It reminds us that an accumulation of student underachievement is based on centuries of neglect and denial of education to entire groups of students (Ladson-Billings 2007). Due to the limitations of isolating academic achievement without an in-depth and robust understanding of the social, cultural, economic, and political histories and relations between African American students and the dominant group, an education debt discourse should replace the achievement gap discourse.

This is the kind of attitudinal reversal that a turnaround principal must have, to reconceptualize the problems of the school in such a way that energizes and potentializes students rather than burdening them with an aura of failure and incompetence. Of course, principals must understand the history of Black education and the harmful effects of white supremacy on students.

Moving to racially conscious action to confront white privilege requires an understanding of race, the history of racial oppression, and one's own identity (Theoharis 2019). This consciousness is a prerequisite to the concrete work of challenging the racial status quo, disrupting white privilege, and undoing racial marginalization in schools, which is such an important part of the turnaround principals' work (Brooks and Theoharis 2019). Without this consciousness, a principal can only maintain the status quo in a turnaround school and continue to offer a flawed educational experience for its students.

Another attitudinal shift is centered on the concept of equality. Some still believe that African American students currently have educational opportunities that are equal to those of white students or any other ethnicity and that success is simply a matter of working hard. But the critically conscious principal will focus on *equity* rather than equality. Equality provides the same resources to all, irrespective of needs or circumstances. Equity seeks to provide resources based on need and circumstances in order that all students have the same shot at equality.

An equitable education is warranted based on the societal challenges that people of color face in comparison with their white counterparts. It recognizes that students attending a turnaround school endure societal challenges that makes survival and obtaining basic needs a priority over an education. A critically conscious principal will understand that these needs are interconnected and that equity must precede equality.

Administrative Factors

A second key factor of critical consciousness is understanding the impact of racist administrative practices on the education of Black students. The critically conscious principal must know the historical and cultural experiences of African Americans and other ethnic student populations in order to properly serve the school community. They are cognizant of African Americans' struggles, one key struggle being the miseducation of African Americans by stripping their minds of self-worth and histories of their own culture.

It is important to understand the education of African American students and any other minority group from a critical lens. The Institute for Multiracial Justice defines white supremacy as "an historically based, institutionally perpetuated system of exploitation and oppression of continents, nations, and peoples of color by white peoples and nations of the European continent, for the purpose of maintaining and defending a system of wealth, power and privilege" (Oakland Unified School District 2020). But the effects of white supremacy are not limited to issues of self-worth and the way Black culture is valued. It is manifested in dozens of administrative practices that harm students.

For example, a vast amount of research shows that too many African American students, especially African American males, are placed in special education programs (Gordon 2017). In addition, African American students are overrepresented in suspension and exclusionary practices, while they are underrepresented in gifted and talented programs, advanced placement courses, and honors classes (Spring 2011).

The disturbing trend of African Americans being ostracized in schools adds to the devaluing of the African American intellect. African American students are suspended at almost four times the rate of white students, are almost three times more likely to be removed from the classroom but kept within the school, and are nearly three times more likely to be expelled from school (Morrison 2019).

African American males with or without disabilities were overrepresented in alternative schools, particularly schools that have been structured with a discipline focus compared with enrollments in nonalternative schools (U.S. Government of Accountability Office 2019). The U.S. Department of Education, National Center for Education Statistics reported, in all years between 2000 and 2016, a higher percentage of African American students were retained (de Brey et al. 2019).

Decades of research have exposed this racial discrimination in schools. The overrepresentation of African American students in the exclusionary disciplinary consequences of suspension and expulsion means that these students are simply not in the classroom as much as their white peers (Fenning and Rose 2007). Students who experience discipline that removes them from the classroom are more likely to repeat a grade, drop out of school, and become involved in the juvenile justice system (U.S. Government Accountability Office 2019).

Furthermore, these persistent trends in schools will have grave impacts on society as a whole since studies have shown that these malicious acts from schools can result in decreased earning potential and added costs to society such as incarceration and lost tax revenue (ibid.). The results of these disparities are tragic. The 2014 Census revealed that more young African American high school dropouts are in prison than employed, which substantiates the proverbial school-to-prison pipeline (Guo 2016).

The school-to-prison pipeline funnels students out of public schools into the juvenile and criminal justice system, despite the fact that many of these students have histories of poverty, abuse, or neglect that affect their progress. These students would benefit from additional educational and counseling services instead of being isolated, punished, and pushed out (American Civil Liberties Union, n.d.).

Pitre (2018) has noted that the standardized testing frenzy may represent a hidden form of racism that has roots in the intelligence tests that were used to label African Americans as inferior. Hours spent preparing for and taking standardized tests may represent hours of self-doubt and judgment. This is another school practice that a critically conscious principal may have to address, making changes in administrative practices that specifically undo this notion and allow students to reject the inferiority message that standardized testing may signal to some.

An awareness of these realities is what can lead the turnaround principal to address head-on these types of discriminatory administrative practices and many others. Critically conscious principals help staff recognize ways in which the school, its culture, and its practices are not race neutral but instead reflect the values of the dominant group (Valles and Miller 2010). Hence, critically conscious leaders ensure that all aspects of the school—the curriculum, culture, structure, and policies—not only reflect the racial diversity of the school but also challenge and eliminate racist assumptions (Capper 2019; Bloom and Erlandson 2003; Wilson and Johnson 2015).

The curriculum is a particularly important element of the school administration that a critically conscious principal will be aware of. For much of its history, Black education has involved celebrating the achievements and greatness of white culture rather than those of African people (Akbar 1996). In schools where this still persists, the principal must address curriculum change.

We now have many decades of research showing how representation matters (Kincheloe and Steinberg 1997; Freire [1970] 2000, as cited in Pitre 2011; Pitre 2015). It is important for African American students to know about their heroes and heroines, scientists, teachers, artists, and inventors, as well as African accomplishments (Akbar 1996). Seeing people who are similar to students is imperative to students believing that they themselves are capable of similar achievements.

The inclusion of African achievement in the curriculum has a parallel in the inclusion of Black teachers and administrators. A 2017 study published by the Institute of Labor Economics found that low-income African American males who were paired with an African American teacher in third, fourth, or fifth grade were 39 percent less likely to drop out of high school (Gershenson et al. 2015). Furthermore, the research found that pairing low-income African American students with at least one African American teacher between third and fifth grades increased their chances to attend a four-year college by 19 percent.

Environmental Factors

A final set of factors that a critically conscious principal must address is environmental factors—meaning all of the factors outside of the school and instruction that will nonetheless impact student learning.

The biggest factor among these is the racial antagonism that fueled American slavery, the Black Codes, Jim Crow, and other forms of post-slavery racism and discrimination that continue to limit the ability of African Americans to dream the American Dream (Horsford 2011). African American students in poor communities may be affected or see neighbors affected by police violence, leading to trauma and mental health challenges.

Kaiser Permanente and the Centers for Disease Control and Prevention conducted the first large-scale study on the relationship between the ten categories of adversity in childhood and health outcomes in adulthood. Adverse childhood experiences (ACEs) are traumatic or stressful events that a child may endure between the ages of birth through seventeen years, such as experiencing violence, abuse, or neglect; witnessing violence in the home or community; or having a family member attempt or die by suicide (Centers for Disease Control and Prevention 2021).

Communities that experience high rates of violence endure an overwhelmingly high rates of trauma (Pinderhughes et al. 2015). Trauma has a significant impact on the development, health, and well-being of children and it's critical to understand that trauma manifests at the community level (ibid.). Additionally, a child's environment can undermine their sense of safety, stability, and bonding if the child grows up in a household with substance misuse, mental health problems, and instability due to parental separation or household members being incarcerated (Centers for Disease Control and Prevention 2021).

These adverse childhood experiences, if not addressed, can be linked to chronic health problems, mental illness, and substance misuse in adulthood along with negatively impacting education and job opportunities (ibid.). The culmination of decades or even centuries of neglect and miseducation are evident in what students observe every day in their community: a school-to-prison pipeline in full operation all around them (Pitre 2014; Alexander 2012). These are students who already suffer disproportionately, such as poverty-stricken students, students of color, English language learners, homeless youth, youth in foster care, and students with disabilities (Kim et al. 2010).

Principals should work with their district to devise strategies to combat the effects of racism on students. Horsford (2011) documents the experience of one superintendent who fought the effects of racism by reminding students that although racism is their reality, it is not their problem—since they could not change it even if they wanted to. This can be a powerful message from a school leader, even if they cannot do anything about the racist actions of others, principals can remind students that they remain disadvantaged by the experience of slavery and discrimination as well as the oppressive mentality of white supremacy (Akbar 1996).

Yet, a student's destiny does not have to be determined by the hatred of others. A critically conscious principal empowers students to dream big regardless of their circumstances. Given the persistence of racism in their lives outside of school, an education with a social justice focus is critical for African American students (Pitre and Smith-Gray 2020). Papa and English (2011) defined social justice as schooling that recognizes and respects the fundamental differences in students' and families' cultural identities and social experiences on the margins of American culture and society and that intentionally attempts to remove barriers that keep them there.

Furman (2012) believes that social justice leadership requires a "heightened and critical awareness of oppression, exclusion, and marginalization" (Brooks and Miles 2006, 5) and a proactive approach to being change agents (Shields 2003). This requires courage and vision for principals since leaders who are viewed as not characteristically following the status quo have been seen as "miscreants" or "troublemakers" (Bogotch 2002; Rapp 2002).

Instead school leaders are often "trained, hired, and rewarded" (230) for maintaining the technical and traditional leadership that has helped sustain an inequitable status quo (Theoharis 2010) within schools that need the most support. The organizational and institutional barriers that contribute to a school's helplessness and inability to effectively serve marginalized communities make bringing about change a monumental task that requires time and sacrifice (DeMatthews 2015). Critically conscious principals must be prepared for a long battle when trying to address these issues.

Racism is a huge factor in students' lives outside of school but not the only one. Economic disadvantages are another environmental factor. A critically conscious principal is aware of this and communicates to teachers and students alike the misunderstanding of meritocracy in culture. Poverty and wealth constitute unearned handicaps and privileges that are passed from one generation to another (Milner 2015). Many times, the lead to opportunities and outcomes that are based not on merit, intelligence, or hard work.

Educators must understand that people growing up in poverty do not generally start their educational or life experience in a fair or equal position (ibid.; Andre-Bechely 2005). All people are created equal, but all people do not have the same opportunities for success. A third environmental factor is more concretely related to "environment"—the physical structures and health concerns that plague the lives of poor students and their families. Children raised in impoverished communities have less opportunites to be exposed to positive life experiences such as visiting parks, zoos, museums, and so on (Jamieson 2020).

The American Academy of Pediatrics endorses an emerging, multidisciplinary science of development that supports an eco-bio-developmental framework, which explains the evolution of early childhood origins of lifelong health and prosperity across the life span (American Academy of Pediatrics 2020). When analyzing the biology of trauma and toxic stress a child may experience, the past few years have brought a dramatic improvement in understanding how a healthy brain develops and the effect, positive or negative, a child's environment has on that process (ibid.).

The prolonged activation of stress response systems can disrupt the brain structure and other organ systems, while further increasing the risk of stress-related disease and cognitive impairment well into the adult years (ibid.). The physical infrastructure may also contribute to learning issues. A child may be exposed to lead paint in old buildings in poor sections of communities. The continued exposure of children to lead paint has a devastating effect on children's development, and these effects can be seen in everything from learning disabilities to female students' rate of teen pregnancy.

Contaminated water systems are an environmental hazard (Lunder 2017). A particularly troublesome example of this is Flint, Michigan, an economically struggling city that is 53 percent African American and has one of the highest poverty rates in the country (Alfonsi 2020). In 2014, the Michigan governor appointed an emergency manager to take over governance of the city, who switched the source of Flint's water supply from the Great Lakes to the Flint River in an attempt to save money.

When it was disclosed in 2015 that lead and other carcinogens were found in the water, Dr. Mona-Hanna-Attisha, who practices at the Hurley Children's Clinic, which serves most of Flint's children, started reviewing blood test results. She estimated that "14,000 kids in Flint under the age of six may have been exposed to lead in their water. Three years after the crisis began, the percentage of third graders in Flint who passed Michigan's standardized literacy test dropped from 41 percent to 10 percent" (ibid.).

Dr. Hanna-Attisha commented on her review of thousands of children's blood test: "I never should have had to do the research that literally used the blood of our children as detectors of environmental contamination." She followed this with in-depth testing of 174 children. The results: "Before the crisis, about 15 percent of the kids in Flint required special education services.

But of the 174 children who went through the extensive neuro-exams, specialists determined that 80 percent will require help for a language, learning or intellectual disorder." And Flint is not an isolated case. Soon after, Newark, New Jersey, had a similar water crisis. As Dr. Hanna-Attisha said, the crisis of water contamination is not a Flint story. "This is an everywhere story. This is an American story."

Critically conscious principals will be aware of all of these types of factors that will affect their students' lives and learning, so that they can advocate for community action as well as for needed supports for children who are affected.

CONCLUSION

A critical consciousness is key for principals of turnaround schools. It is only with a critical consciousness of race and socioeconomics that a principal can have a vision of what students really need and be able to communicate that vision to students, staff, and district administrators alike. Such a principal will be aware of all the factors that impact education in their school—attitudinal factors, administrative factors, and environmental factors.

As the United States sees the continued "browning" of our schools, the status quo concerning school leadership, curriculum, and pedagogy must be challenged (Anyon 1997; Carlson and Apple 1998; Darling-Hammond 2019; Delpit 1995; Dimitriadis and Carlson 2003, as cited in Dantley 2005). The National Center for Education Statistics (McFarland et al. 2019) predicted that the percentage of white students enrolled in public schools between 2015 and 2027 will continue to decrease from 49 percent to 45 percent, while the number of Hispanic students would increase from 26 percent to 29 percent and African American student numbers are projected to remain stable at 15 percent.

Principals with a critical consciousness will be key to educating these students in a way that unleashes their potential (Pitre and Smith-Bryant 2020). Dantley (2010) stated that transformative leaders permit their spiritual selves to assist with the execution of leadership responsibilities. He understood that transformative leaders use their inner strength to resist both the systematic inequities in the educational system and the hegemonic structures and forms of oppression running rampant in society.

He argued that the perceptions of these leaders should move beyond proficiencies and minimum competencies and instead focus on ontological pursuits, academic and intellectual engagements, and projects fostering students' sense of destiny, purpose, and commitment to societal change. Most important, the critically conscious principal is characterized by an understanding that educational inequities exist not because of students, families, or communities but as a result of the structural, historical inequalities in society and schools (Bloom and Erlandson 2003).

An urban school district's prominent leader once stated, "As long as we remain focused on supporting students, all else will fall into place." Therefore, creating a student-centered learning environment evolves into providing resources that fit student circumstances and helping students overcome any specific challenges that impede education. In this way, a critically conscious principal who takes the helm of a low-performing school can "turn around" not only the students' achievement but the harms done through the attitudinal, administrative, and environmental factors that have compromised the education of African American and other marginalized students.

These leaders advocate for students above and beyond their role and responsibilities because they reject students' failure. Critically conscious principals never conform to the status quo because they firmly believe in students' potential and diligently work to help others see the true potential in students as well. To empower future leaders of the world means more than being a school administrator, teacher, school counselor, or a social worker; it means altering the trajectory of students who deserve quality education regardless of their skin color. Critically conscious leaders liberate students based on their own consciousness of racial disparities and refuse to allow the stigma of a turnaround school to thwart their students' potential and bright futures.

Chapter 4

The Critically Conscious Principal in Action

Too many students in K-12 institutions have not been provided an opportunity to develop into successful students because the educational system has not been structurally designed for them to do so (Milner 2010). Massive federal funding and unreasonable timetables for change have often failed to turn around struggling schools, but there is hope in the employment of principals who are critically conscious to provide the missing piece of the turnaround puzzle.

A critically conscious principal will be aware of the ways in which history and present-day realities affect the success of their students, including attitudinal factors like hopelessness, administrative factors like biased suspension and expulsion trends, and environmental factors like adverse childhood and community experiences, like lead paint and water poisoning, as well as systemic racism. This chapter dives deeper into the role of such a principal, showing what concrete steps may be taken and what research reveals about practices rooted in a critical consciousness of race and power.

WHY PRINCIPALS MATTER

Over forty years of evidence suggest that effective school leaders drastically influence student achievement and aspects of school performance (Steiner et al. [2008] 2016). Grissom et al. (2021) discovered that effective principals have positive impacts on student achievement and attendance, as well as teacher satisfaction and retention. The new research showed how the importance of principals may not have been stated strongly enough in earlier work, given the magnitude and scope of the principal's work.

The principals' effects on students are considerably indirect, whereas the principals' influence on teachers and their development directly creates conditions for sound learning (Grissom et al. 2021). Effective principals make certain to position their practice toward instruction focused on interactions with teachers, building productive school climates, facilitating collaboration and professional learning communities, and strategic personnel and resource management processes.

Research on principals in turnaround schools in particular, is still scant. Most research paradigms focus on results and not on the internal issues of the leader's beliefs and values (English 2008). Some of the literature on school turnaround fails to deal with the essential inner core of leaders who successfully turn around low-performing schools (English and Papa 2010). There should be mass research exploring the countless stories and experiences of turnaround principals, as opposed to the current focus on turnaround students' metrics.

When a principal leads a school from disaster to improvement, it is a rare phenomenon, and we need to understand deeply what made that success possible. There is some research on principalship in struggling schools; however, a review of empirical studies on school leadership by Myers and Hambrick Hitt (2017) revealed that nearly every study recognized the turnaround principal as being responsible for shifting the mindset of teachers and setting clear expectations, in which teachers should believe that their students can learn regardless of their backgrounds and circumstances.

Meyers and Hambrick Hitt reviewed eighteen empirical studies that categorized areas of educational leadership in which turnaround principals should excel while also highlighting the limited evidence on attitudes, traits, and perspectives that they should possess. The emerging evidence suggests that turnaround principals are fundamentally different from other effective principals, but the Meyers and Hambrick Hitt review is short on details about the specific competencies that make an effective turnaround leader. The following sections suggest important ways that principals can transform their schools based on an understanding of critical consciousness.

ENSURING CULTURALLY RELEVANT CURRICULA AND MULTICULTURAL EDUCATION PRACTICES

Principals must develop an equity lens, particularly as they meet the needs of growing numbers of marginalized students (Grissom et al. 2021). One of the key ways that a principal can use their critical consciousness to help turnaround schools is through the curriculum. The most straightforward aspect of this is to be sure that curricula feature the diaspora of African American or Latinx, not just of white Europeans or Americans.

While Black History Month was a good start, figures from marginalized communities need to be part of the curriculum year-round. Critical consciousness encompasses an understanding of the historical, political, economic, and social role of education in maintaining oppressive structures (Pitre 2015). Therefore, the curriculum has to begin with educating African Americans and other minority ethnic students about the history of their race and culture as well as topics like human potential, evolutionary psychology, and the origin of mental structures (Pitre 2018).

Some schools have adopted an African-centered curriculum to radically address the cultural irrelevance of their previous curricula. Whether using an African-centered curriculum or not, we must shift the curriculum from an excessive and distorted focus on white people and expand on the cultural history of African Americans (Akbar 1996). This will foster what Asante (2003) recognized as a two-prong approach to consciousness-raising: being able to articulate one's oppression and also recognizing one's own potential to be free, resilient, and victorious.

A more complex aspect of curriculum reform is disrupting the deceitful portrayal of American history that is taught daily to most students. Many teachers are unprepared to do this because they received the same fraudulent perspective of America's history that their students receive today; they just don't have the knowledge of racism and oppression that affects students' lives, as well.

The Southern Poverty Law Center determined that schools are not adequately teaching the history of American slavery; educators are not sufficiently prepared to teach it, nor do textbooks have enough information about the hard reality of slavery (Shuster 2018). Often textbooks condense the history of twenty-five decades of enslavement of African Americans into one chapter, painting a static picture of a time allegedly disconnected with the present (Baptist 2014).

Making sure that students understand this history can be tricky. Some teachers may not be comfortable leading discussions on the topic. Some other teachers may attempt to educate students about the harsh reality of the slave trade and the making of American capitalism but may fail to grasp how many African American students struggle with shame about their ancestors' suffering (Baptist 2014).

Finding a way to teach this history, fully but sensitively, is crucial. We must remember that we are in a country that was economically propelled on the back of African slavery. Without this authentic understanding of a painful past, African American students will struggle to be liberated and empowered because they are deprived of knowing their history, culture, and identity. They need the knowledge of the systems and structures that create and sustain inequity (a matter of critical analysis) to develop a sense of power or capability (a matter of agency) and to commit to act against oppressive conditions (El-Amin et al. 2017).

The implementation of multicultural education in African American schools is key. An antiracist educational curriculum is one in which educators create learning environments, as Ibram Kendi stated, "the cultures and ways of life of different groups of people are valued and taught and understood equally . . . A learning environment where Black doesn't mean 'misbehaving' " (Koenig 2020).

It will include elements of the painful reality of American history as well as a celebration of Black achievement. Kendi (2019) stated, "the only way to undo racism is to consistently identify and describe it—and then dismantle it." Likewise, educators should make majoritarian students aware of their own cultural lenses and allow them to see that a curriculum may be biased and have a certain cultural arbitrariness embedded within it (Papa and English 2011).

Furthermore, the employment of educators who resemble the students is critical to students' development. As an African American, the experience of being taught by African American educators and leaders from elementary to high school helped develop a consciousness of societal norms. Creating diverse and inclusive learning environments helps develop and prepare students for a diverse society. Numerous research studies state that African American students perform better in school when they have been taught by an African American.

Tomorrow's classrooms are already becoming more racially diverse, and efforts to increase diverse educators in schools will be imperative. School principals working to transform predominantly African American schools should be aware of how schools continue a long historical tradition of serving the interest of the ruling elite (Pitre 2015). Effective turnaround principals create school communities that demolish this tradition and embrace the cultural differences of the school with helping teachers embed diversity and inclusion lessons and activities into the classroom setting, engaging students from their cultural lens.

MAKING ROOM FOR STUDENT AGENCY AND VOICES

African American and Latinx representation in the curricula is just one aspect of critical curriculum-building. Another is to find ways to incorporate students' experiences and voices as an integral part of their education. Just as scholars learn from experts or researchers in the education field, we must learn from our students. Research indicates that students who believe they have a voice in school are seven times more likely to be academically motivated than students who do not believe they have a voice (Quaglia Institute for School Voice and Aspirations 2016).

Allowing students to communicate their experiences in the classroom gives teachers, other students, and even the students themselves a chance to truly grasp the challenges in their lives (Kim 2015). Principals can help provide tools to teachers to achieve this kind of open and holistic communication. Creating restorative justice circles (Boyes-Watson and Pranis 2015) or embedding the collaborative problem solving (CPS) approach in the classroom to listen to and reflect on students' narratives is a step in the right direction.

A restorative practice circle provides a safe place for students to express themselves. The circle is designed as a highly structured intentional space to encourage connection, understanding, and dialogue in a group setting that is strictly voluntary. It allows students and adults to slow down and be in the present, enter a space of equality where the structure of power in schools' hierarchy is not recognized, speak from the heart and deal with emotions, and prioritize building relationships. It can be used after an upsetting incident or even just when the classroom atmosphere has gotten tense.

A circle works in several defined steps. The leader of the circle—the "circle keeper"—opens the circle by expressing a welcoming into the space of the circle, conducting a mindfulness moment, explaining why participants are there, and introducing of the concept of "rounds." They then conduct the rounds and finally close with a check-out round and final reflections (Boyce-Watson and Pranis 2015).

The mindfulness moment gives participants a moment to pause, breathe, and listen to the sounds around them—to ground themselves in the present moment rather than living in a past moment of conflict. The rounds consist of questions that are asked of the participants with the understanding that each participant will receive the talking piece (an object of some sort) that gives them "the floor"—the right to speak while others listen without interrupting. The circle is voluntary, so a participant may always pass the talking piece if they do not want to speak during a round.

The circle approach recognizes the importance of relationships in human development, and learning and can be an important part of a school-wide approach to restorative practices, which include positive discipline (not punitive), trauma-sensitive learning environments, and the use of mindfulness practices (Boyes-Watson and Pranis 2015). The most important factor in a circle's success is the attitude of the classroom teachers. They must believe in the process and (ibid.) understand how giving students a voice can unlock their potential.

Kim (2015) wrote, "theory devoid of lived experiences would be like an empty tin can that just makes noise" (41). Textbook solutions for student misbehavior may be fine for an average school, but turnaround schools need more. Making students' stories and voices a part of their education honors the lived experiences of students as a source of important knowledge and understanding (Boyd 2009; Martin 1986, as cited in Kim 2015).

It liberates students by homing in to their previously untapped and unacknowledged expertise and knowledge thus giving them an alternative way of knowing and accessing historical truths (Kim 2015). Also, it gives meaning to the experience of going to school, making it a place where important stories are told and truths that are relevant to their lives are unfolded (Clandinin 2013). While students' narratives about their lived experiences are valuable in general, they are particularly valuable when it comes to their schooling.

Turnaround principals who engage the student population to share their good or bad educational experiences respect what students have to say about their own journey of learning. This can give teachers and principals insight into what motivates (or demotivates) students, what hidden struggles they wrestle with, and what they consider to be obstacles or supports to their education.

While principals may gather helpful instructional insight, allowing students to contribute to the shape and content of their education has benefits that are far more important than any classroom tips that may be gleaned. When students are able to give their perspective on their education to a receptive audience of teachers and administrators, it conveys a sense of empowerment and agency. It models for them that they have a right to shape the society that in turn shapes them. It communicates that things can change and that they—the students—can have a hand in making those changes happen.

EMPHASIZING RELATIONSHIP-BUILDING

Dr. Linda Darling-Hammond stated that "strong relationships are central to the learning process" (Edutopia 2019). Far from being a nicety or secondary attribute of good teaching, developing positive relationships with students is the bedrock of teaching, the piece that makes everything else possible, especially in a turnaround school.

A principal can teach their teachers about practical strategies like the Collaborative Problem Solving® (CPS) approach. Developed by doctors at Massachusetts General Hospital and the Harvard Medical School, CPS was designed to help children and teachers regulate their emotions and actions, relate to one another, and use reason and thoughtfulness to address their issues (Think:Kids, n.d.). The developers realized that students with challenging behaviors are often tragically misunderstood and wanted to develop a more compassionate and effective approach to behavioral problems.

CPS involves meeting with a student who is having trouble in the classroom. The teacher is first tasked with really listening to the student's view of their educational experience and even of the teacher themselves. The teacher actively listens, shows empathy, and then shares their own concerns. This exchange of perspectives on an equal footing will help build a relationship between the teacher and student that culminates in inviting the student to come up with ways to address both of their issues. A dedicated structure for engaging students to tell their own stories is a worthwhile addition to the school day.

But the initial step is to connect and build a genuine relationship with all students, listening and hearing from one another. Principals can encourage teachers to embrace the complexity of students' experiences rather than assigning simple explanations or categories to their lives (Creswell and Poth 2018). When principals help teachers understand all the complex external environmental factors and community adversities that students sometimes endure, teachers will have a better, more empathetic understanding of students' behaviors in the school setting.

Merely categorizing students as "at-risk" or "high fliers" overly simplifies their situation; taking a deep dive into their cultures and lives is one way to connect with students and listening to their narratives. This empathy is not a pie-in-the-school, feel-good fantasy for school improvement. Spark (2019) analyzed forty-six studies on the topic of teacher–student relationships and found that strong teacher–student relationships were associated with short- and long-term improvements in student academic engagement, attendance, and grades as well as with fewer disruptive behaviors, fewer suspensions, and lower dropout rates.

Critically conscious turnaround principals must be cognizant of the power of relationships. They must diligently work to create school communities that have a foundation of strong and respectful relationships with teachers, students, families, and the community. It's one of the most powerful things they can do.

PRIORITIZING INSTRUCTIONAL TIME

A critically conscious principal will pay attention to the quantity of instruction as well as the quality. We know that African American students spend less time getting instruction than white counterparts because of disciplinary policies (Spring 2011). The UCLA Civil Rights Project released a national analysis of how disparate school discipline continues to drive differences in the opportunity to learn when the U.S. Department of Education revealed that a total of 11,392,474 million instructional days were lost during the 2015–2016 school year in May of 2020 (Losen and Martinez 2021).

Taking a closer look at the disparities, African American students lost 103 days per 100 students enrolled, 82 more days than the 21 days that white students lost due to out-of-school suspensions (ibid.). Furthermore, African American males had the highest rate and African American females had the second highest rate at 75 days per 100 students enrolled (ibid.).

Classroom instruction is already under undue pressure. Instructional time has only worsened when the school culture is one that emphasizes meetings and endless discussion that don't result in concrete action. Educators in low-performing schools are all too familiar with the magnitude of scheduled or emergency meetings announced throughout the week. Many times leadership teams, professional learning committees, school improvement teams, family care units, and school improvement subcommittees require teachers and student services support personnel to divert their time and energies from instruction to repetitive meetings.

Turnaround principals must be conscious of the number of meetings held throughout the school and value the need for teachers and other pertinent members of the school community to plan for instruction. The best committee work in the world is in vain if teachers and staff have no time to implement their findings and suggestions.

ATTENDING TO MENTAL HEALTH

Hard as it is to believe, frequently a turnaround principal is placed or recruited to a turnaround school without any knowledge of what the school's needs really are. A school's status may be measured by student metrics like graduation rates and standardized testing, but these metrics don't adequately convey the needs of the school.

One factor affecting the students may be mental health issues. Students coming from underserved communities endure chronic trauma and stress. The trauma and stress are devastating to students' ability to learn. The turnaround principal must be aware of student needs and be ready to plan with student support services and external behavioral and mental health agencies to supply the mental health services that some of their students desperately need. Addressing the mental health needs and including social–emotional learning into the school community must be a priority when discussing transformation of a turnaround school.

Students with untreated trauma or stress experience learning problems with lower grades and suspensions and expulsions (SAMHSA 2015). In Maslow's hierarchy of needs, survival and safety come first. If an individual is in a constant state of crisis regarding these basic needs, the higher strata of Maslow's hierarchy like esteem and self-actualization will be abandoned. In addition, constant stress affects people's physiology.

For students, stress and trauma may lead to problems like having nightmares, difficulty concentrating, difficulty sleeping, being depressed or feeling lonely, and so on (SAMHSA 2015). Elevated cortisol levels cause students to have a fight-or-flight mentality, creating social and behavioral problems. It affects memory and learning, as it diverts energy from higher functions to basic physiological systems.

If mental health and social–emotional needs are not addressed, the classroom setting will be devoid of learning. Turnaround principals must have a sense of how many of their students are affected by stress, trauma, and other mental health issues. If turnaround principals are going to bring about transformation to a struggling school community, knowing the students and communities being served on a personal level is imperative.

They may start by noticing the severity of students' toxic stress and mental health challenges during bus and hallway duties and critiques of suspension data. Observing student behaviors in the cafeteria, bus parking lot, hallways, and so on is eye-opening; students' interactions with peers and adults provide a wealth of information which is often overlooked. Students do not misbehave or act out deliberately or intentionally; there is always an underlying concern that needs to be unpacked and addressed in a restorative and healing manner by principals.

Consulting and contracting with mental health organizations or local mental health clinics to understand the neuroscience of trauma and toxic stress is one way to begin changing the school climate for the betterment of the students. Utilizing school funding to contract with external mental health agencies or local hospitals with proven results in the community is imperative, because most educators are not experts in the mental health field. For turnaround schools, based on the community adversities of many students, it is better to contract the services inside the school versus relying on families to take students to the services.

Principals must identify the students with the highest number of behavioral infractions or suspension incidents and start building a relationship with the families. The importance of warm interpersonal relationships with the families of students cannot be overstated. The relationship will be critical when obtaining consent from parents to provide necessary supports to heal the unaddressed mental health struggles of their child(ren).

It's important to recognize, too, that students are not the only ones affected by mental health. Recognizing teachers' mental health challenges is vital. The pedagogy within the classroom can be compromised because of teachers' struggles. Teachers may feel burned out from the workload. They may have experienced trauma at the school or in the community. They may be overwhelmed by trying to help their students or by simply observing their students' struggles. And they may battle classroom dysfunction and behavioral problems.

Or they may simply experience chronic stress from trying to keep up with the demands that are made of staff in turnaround schools. When teachers receive demands from principals or instructional coaches to promptly increase students' academic proficiency, their ability to do so can mean the difference between having a job and not having a job. This is the frightening reality for educators in the twenty-first century.

It is particularly frightening for teachers who realize that the students that they are now responsible for have not yet mastered previous academic standards. Often teachers and administrators will engage in "social promotion," where a student is promoted to the next grade despite the teacher realizing the student has not mastered the current grade's content. Once promoted to the next grade, the new teacher is held responsible for the students' progress. This can increase an overwhelming anxiety response for teachers and contribute to the challenges of working in a turnaround school.

Turnaround principals must be prepared to address *all* the needs of their school community. Mental health needs cannot be ignored. If so, the turnaround principal can expect to have a short-lived tenure and become part of the educational stress machine as high turnover rates continue.

REPLACING PUNITIVE DISCIPLINE WITH RESTORATIVE JUSTICE DISCIPLINE

There is a substantial amount of research surrounding the connections between race, poverty, student behavior, and suspension/expulsion. Disciplinary practices toward African American students in schools directly link their educational experiences, whether positive or negative, to their life trajectories. Every year, large numbers of African American students are steered away from the classroom into the criminal justice system (Quereshi and Okonofua 2017).

Psychologists are starting to understand that the high levels of discipline of African American students stems from a two-way social–psychological dynamic between teachers and students, resulting in stereotyping and bias (Quereshi and Okonofua 2017). Implicit bias manifests itself in schools and is directly relevant to discipline in the classroom, but the principal is the one to ultimately determine how a child will be disciplined. Many principals fall into the trap of trying to follow board policies that are punitive instead of restorative and that are designed to satisfy the teachers' desire to have a student removed from the classroom.

It's important to understand that school discipline is linked to later consequences, and studies have found that students assigned to high suspension schools are more likely to be arrested and incarcerated later in life and less likely to attend a four-year college (Boudreau 2019). School discipline or pushing a student out of the classroom or school setting is not the answer.

The Center for Promise, a research institute of America's Promise Alliance, analyzed how and why students are disconnected from school after facing harsh disciplinary actions (Luster 2018). The executive director, Dr. Jonathan Zaff, stated, "The reality is that exclusionary discipline practices do not make schools more conducive to learning, do not help improve student behavior, and do not make schools safer" (ibid.).

In 2014, the Obama administration issued the first national guidance on school discipline, advising schools to limit suspensions and other practices that remove students from the classroom (U.S. Department of Education 2014). However, only four years later, the Trump administration's Department of Justice and Department of Education issued a joint statement with Betsy DeVos rescinding Obama's guidance to reduce racial discrimination in school discipline (Kamenetz 2018).

These racial discriminatory practices toward African American children are in direct alignment with mass incarceration of the African American. Severe exclusionary disciplinary practices disrupt learning and create disconnected students, making them feel undervalued, unwelcome, and misunderstood (Luster 2018). The damaging long-lasting effects of zero tolerance sparked a movement for many schools to transition from these practices to focus more on social–emotional learning, restorative practices, and positive behavior interventions (Luster 2018).

With racial tensions from police brutality toward African Americans sweeping throughout the country, schools must rethink disciplinary practices. One movement and alternative to suspension and expulsion is school-based restorative practices. Restorative discipline and conflict circles can be one way a school community can begin to repair the harm done to African American students in the form of suspensions and expulsions.

These practices can include the restorative circles described earlier, teaching mindfulness exercises, allowing students a chance to be heard through storytelling, and developing a plan and an agreement to move past the conflict. There is a growing body of research on the effectiveness of school-based restorative justice in reducing suspensions, expulsions, and police referrals while improving academic outcomes for students and reducing violence (Davis 2019).

In a study on school-wide restorative justice in Oakland, California, from 2011 to 2014, graduation rates in schools with restorative practices increased by 60 percent compared to a 7 percent increase in nonrestorative schools;

reading scores increased 128 percent versus 11 percent; and the dropout rate decreased 56 percent versus 17 percent (ibid.). Harm was repaired by 76 percent in conflict circles, with students learning to talk instead of fight through differences at home or school (ibid.).

More importantly, more than 88 percent of teachers stated that restorative practices were very or somewhat helpful in managing difficult student behaviors (ibid.). Restorative schools are vested in repairing the harm of the student or adult, but the use of restorative discipline is effective only if there is a school-wide approach that rests on shared aspiration to build a caring school community (Boyes-Watson and Pranis 2015).

A restorative justice approach to discipline has proved so successful that the Minnesota Department of Education developed the *Restorative Practices Implementation Guidance* to help school districts and schools to integrate restorative practices into school-wide climates, disciplines, equity, and teaching and learning practices (Minnesota Department of Education, n.d.).

The Minnesota Department of Education consults with and provides guidance to other school districts to help educational leaders confront district officials tasked with writing board policies regarding discipline. Principals must create school-level reports and data reviews in which discipline issues surface so leaders may establish data-driven goals to change and heal the school community with restorative practices.

The California Department of Education has also found a way to keep more students in school instead of relying on punitive discipline practices that take students out of the classroom. Specifically, in Oakland, California, strategic and purposeful planning has occurred to educate schools and school districts on restorative justice practices since research on student engagement, academic success, and dropout and graduation rates has shown the need to replace punitive disciplinary practices (California Department of Education 2020).

For this reason, some schools are becoming more restorative and trauma-informed to help change, heal, and restore academic outcomes for their students. With the COVID-19 pandemic, restorative and trauma-informed schools will be even more urgently needed to support returning students and teachers that have endured chronic stress from limited social interaction and learning.

Principals, specifically turnaround principals who normally have high suspension levels, must rethink how discipline is orchestrated in the school, then educate staff on racial justice and healing to build a restorative school community. They must create a positive climate in which all members, including students, experience a sense of belonging and respect; the investment of building healthy relationships will not be in vain when things go wrong (Boyes-Watson and Pranis 2015).

When students do not feel heard or understood, they check out or disconnect from the school and their future; this result is terrible and unnecessary (Luster 2018). Turnaround principals who are critically conscious understand the healing that is needed in schools and work diligently to repair the harm of racial injustices of school discipline.

CRAFTING APPROPRIATE PROFESSIONAL DEVELOPMENT OF STAFF

A final issue that critically conscious principals must address is the preparation of staff for working in a turnaround school. Many educators struggle because they have learned teaching strategies from textbooks but have no real idea of their students' needs and experiences. The majority of students in turnaround schools have endured traumatic life experiences at an early age. Teachers from outside the community may have no idea that these traumas have occurred, much less what the fallout might be.

This leads to a major problem in turnaround schools because teachers have to be able to relate to their students or at least be empathetic to their needs. Without understanding students' trials and tribulations, teachers will struggle to connect genuinely with students in turnaround schools. Because of this, a major concern for principals is determining the professional development needed for teachers and shifting the mindsets of teachers who may see students as lazy.

The same way that teachers have to reteach foundational content to struggling students, many educators have to be reoriented to the realities of their students' lives that might cause them to struggle in school. They must be willing to comprehend the societal injustices that underserved students and families face, such as food and shelter insecurities, fear of living in a community of crime and violence, or daily exposure or consumption of toxic chemicals that damage developing brain cells and cause short- and long-term effects to the body.

If a teacher has a persistent difficulty understanding the struggles of the students and families served, then educating in a low-performing school is not the right place for that individual. These struggles and challenges of underserved communities are excessive, and school personnel, especially the turnaround principal, must have a will to educate *all* children. Another issue is the concentration of subpar teachers in turnaround schools. Many educators entered the field of education because they have an authentic heart for children and want to change the academic outcomes of students.

But some educators have settled in the field and entered the "lemon dance," in which schools habitually transfer their lowest-performing educator to another school, often a low-performing school. Turnaround schools often receive ineffective teachers who have been rejected by other schools, but these schools cannot afford faulty personnel. Ineffective teachers only strengthen the contribution of failed outcomes over a long period of time. Turnaround principals must launch interventions to improve these teachers as well as find ways to bring the best and the brightest to their schools.

Hiring talented teachers in turnaround schools can be difficult but not impossible. School districts with low-performing schools that eventually had successful outcomes aggressively recruited, hired, and trained teachers who displayed resilience, hard work, the ability to work with diverse populations, had high-quality instruction, and had high expectations for students during their in-person interview (Straus and Miller 2016).

Also, one turnaround school's approach to hiring talented teachers required teachers to teach a lesson, submit a lesson plan, and share an artifact with how they previously used student achievement data to progress monitor and differentiate instruction (ibid.). In turnaround schools, an additional step has been taken to improve classroom teaching through instructional coaching programs in which the strengthening of the teacher pipeline occurs (ibid.)

The creation of professional learning communities led by an instructional leader to receive one-on-one coaching involved the review of data to make informed decisions on pedagogy, the analysis of students' work, and building upon teachers' understanding of Common Core standards (ibid.). This kind of effective professional development for teachers is imperative for teachers' learning and refining the pedagogies required to teach the complex skills that students need for further education and work in the twenty-first century (Darling-Hammond et al. 2017).

The root of unpreparedness, when it occurs, lies with teachers' own education. Only a handful of colleges and universities are stepping up to revise education programs and courses of studies to educate prospective teachers on racial and social injustices in education. Teaching current and future educators about how to help struggling students is key to restoring our most challenging schools. Universities and colleges of education must teach educators the damage that results from teaching all students from a Eurocentric lens.

In order to address the underlying foundation of racism in educational leadership programs, Gooden and Dantley (2012) stressed the importance of promoting a "transgressive agenda aimed at transforming the ways, attitudes, and structures that have for so long propagated a racist, classist, and sexist ideology" (243, as cited in Brooks and Theoharis 2019). Without a racially literate understanding of why educational inequities and injustices exist in the first place, teachers, educational leaders, policymakers, and scholars alike will be hard-pressed in any effort to resist and transform the educational structures and systems that reproduce and maintain the unequal inputs and outcomes that warrant disruption (Horsford 2011).

Historically, universities and colleges of education have been vital members when discussing how to prepare pre-service and in-service educators. Therefore, future teachers and educational leaders who are or will be entrusted to serving children and families must be racially literate (ibid.). Universities and colleges of education have a responsibility to prepare future educators by implementing critical dialogues on structural and systemic racism, microaggressions, and implicit and explicit biases within specific courses as well as establishing field assignments and experiences for students.

The field of education continues and will forever change based on the multiculturalism of the world, global fluctuations, and the needs of specific communities. For schools to educate future leaders to be globally competitive, reforming the educational landscape is a must. A conscious effort to prepare, educate, and train teachers on new pedagogical strategies that accelerate learning to students as well as changing mindsets from previous implicit biases that spread into the learning environment is critical.

Once teachers have graduated and entered the job market, it is the job of the principal to keep an eye on the performance of the staff. Like eagles soaring in the sky to survey the landscape for prey, turnaround principals must be always watching out for performance issues and teacher needs. Addressing biased mindsets and subpar teaching may require the hiring of experts who can challenge irrelevant textbook practices, offer insight about multiculturalism and culturally relevant or social justice pedagogy, and work with traumatized populations.

They may offer unique professional development opportunities geared toward the particular challenges of turnaround schools. Culturally relevant professional development may be needed to help teachers who are connecting with students daily from different backgrounds and ethnicities. The professional development in a turnaround school must match the student needs along with teacher needs.

For turnaround schools, good professional development is a non-negotiable. Learning about, applying, and being held accountable to implement best practices should be demanded of all stakeholders. Even though change can be challenging and overwhelming for some educators, providing relevant professional development based on the needs of the school community cannot be circumvented. It may be tempting to bring in the kind of professional development that is popular in other schools but that may not be appropriate for a turnaround school.

Therefore, principals must vet all types of professional development that are offered and be sure to bring in programs that have evidence-based results. Getting the input from all the stakeholders is important to the process as well. Principals must also embrace—and communicate to teachers—the truth that teachers from all walks of life can be effective teachers to students in turnaround schools. If teachers care about students genuinely and empathetically and are willing to learn, they can have great success. Critically conscious turnaround principals will make sure that they have the tools to do so.

MAKING LEADERSHIP WORK FOR PRINCIPALS

As we've seen, principals can make a drastic difference in their schools if they are equipped with the right skills and a critical consciousness of race and wealth. But principals are only human; they need support to bring their visions to light and to survive the challenges of one of the toughest jobs in all of American education. Here are some ways principals can be supported.

The high turnover rate of principals in turnaround schools is a major issue in American education. Principals are often assigned to lead a turnaround school based on their success with non-turnaround schools. But the two types of school are in no way comparable, and the role of the principal is many times more complex in a turnaround school. Turnaround schools on the high school level are often known as "dropout factories" because less than 60 percent of freshman remain four years later.

New principals arriving in a turnaround school have an enormous challenge and often have to clean up the messes left behind by other administrators. How well they clean them up will determine the sustainability of their job. One way to make principals' jobs easier is to abandon the wholesale social promotion of students throughout elementary and middle school. There may be many reasons why teachers may choose social promotion even when they know a student is not prepared for the next grade level.

Part of the principal's job will be, first, to understand why the student is not prepared. Did teachers fail to engage the student? Did they get to know the student on a deeper and genuine level to unravel any hidden neglect or abuse? Was the student habitually suspended? Does the student have health issues that complicate their learning? These are all things a principal should investigate and address with other stakeholders.

Once the cause of the student being unprepared is determined, there is still the issue of whether to promote them or not. Often times, the student will be promoted to the next grade level because of their age or parents' demands, but the principal's duty is to recognize deficiencies of students, empower teachers to reeducate students with necessary foundational skills, and liberate students' self-worth and development. Having students repeat a grade in order to gain mastery over the material is necessary and mandatory if the turnaround principal wants to make a difference in the school community and, more importantly, make a difference in a child's life.

Another change that district administrators can make is to recognize the time required to make progress in a turnaround school. Addressing countless issues within the first two to three years and staying focused on the initial vision of transforming a turnaround school is a daunting task. If change is not forthcoming quickly, there may be notifications from district offices to the turnaround principal's desk that recommend resignation, termination, or retirement after only a short time.

These threats fail to acknowledge the many obstacles a turnaround principal will face and the research that real change within an organization normally requires three to five years. Effective turnaround leaders need this time to build trust with faculty and parents, implement a vision for improvement, and hire talented people; however, many principals in low-performing schools leave before sustaining change (Tyre 2015).

Solving the rapid turnover rates of turnaround principals is key. A Brookings Institution study showed that, in North Carolina, about one-third of the lowest-performing schools lose their principal in any given year (Harbatkin and Henry 2019). A 2017 national survey found that 18 percent of public-school principals left their position, and in high-poverty schools the turnover rate was 21 percent (Levin et al. 2019).

In Chicago Public Schools, among forty-two principals at the eighteen turnaround schools, ten principals left within a year of the turnaround itself or of taking over leadership at the school, and eleven principals left after two to three years (Harris 2014). The high turnover has ripple effects, leading to increased teacher turnover rates, negative effects on students' outcomes, and poor morale within the school community.

The turnover rate of principals can align with teacher turnover rates, which creates instability and jeopardizes school improvement (Levin et al. 2019). I worked in a turnaround school that had four principals in a four-year span. Ultimately, the school was closed. The "closure model" of the ARRA specifies that students should be sent to a well-performing school, but the students were simply shuffled to a nearby struggling school. Unfortunately, many students were lost in the transition and dropped out of school.

Support from the community helps turnaround schools greatly with respect to moving the principals' vision forward. In order for key stakeholders to buy-in to the turnaround principal's vision, it is essential for community partners to understand the goals for the school. Stakeholders respect authentic communication. When serving a community that has already witnessed trials and tribulations, there is a moral responsibility to share strengths and weaknesses of the school community in order for critical dialogues to develop into action steps. Being transparent about expectations and the specific areas for improvement should be communicated with compassion and resilience.

Internal and external stakeholders can support the efforts of the school to make do with limited resources and funding experiences. External stakeholders are extremely helpful to the success of the turnaround school. There are many ways for the community to support turnaround schools and vice versa. Examples may include partnering with local Walmart to set up a stuff-the-bus event with consumers supplying school supplies for students and teachers with a school bus parked in front of the business; local small businesses or corporations providing internships or job shadowing; or churches and YMCAs helping with donations, school supplies, tutorials, lunch buddies, and so on.

Many turnaround schools cannot survive without the help of the community. This kind of external support also gives the principal a feeling of hope and potential that may be the difference between continuity in leadership or another visionary leader falling into the turnover trap.

CONCLUSION

The figure of the principal is one of the most influential factors in school success. For a turnaround school, having a critically conscious principal is key. Their critical consciousness allows them to see and address issues like a culturally relevant curriculum, mental health services for students, excessive and biased disciplinary action, and professional development needs that are unique to the turnaround school setting.

Schools notice reform when multiple elements to improve schools are in place, such as strong school leadership, links to parents and the community, development of teachers' professional capacity, a safe and stimulating learning climate, and instructional guidance and materials (Bryk et al. 2010; David 2010). But principals can only work in pursuit of their vision for the school if they are not burned out or discouraged and when they are given the appropriate time to make it happen. In carrying out the vision of a just and inclusive education, the district and the community have a part too.

Chapter 5

Lessons Learned from Critically Conscious Leaders

Principals appear to be the most crucial element in school turnaround efforts. While all principals need leadership and administrative skills, turnaround principals in particular need a critical consciousness of race and wealth inequality. The poor communities where turnaround schools are located add severe challenges to students' education, and only a critically conscious principal can be aware of those challenges and reflect that awareness in their policies and approach to school issues. This might be as simple as including more minority figures in the curriculum or as complex as incorporating student feedback and life experiences in the school day.

But principals' jobs are made harder by some of the persistent problems in school districts. Communities and sometimes even staff have a dismal view of the turnaround schools' prospects. Even schools with some record of improvement are usually unable to sustain that success as funding peters out and staff is shuffled from school to school. By the time the special turnaround funding ends, some of the consequences of unwanted change—like the heavy emphasis on standardized testing, traumatic shifts in school culture, and teachers burned out from the stress of meeting metric goals—have begun to manifest.

School turnaround is a complex problem. But the main issue with turnaround schools is the lack of sustaining the improvements and the continued presence of the turnaround principal who enhanced the school into a well-developed learning community. When we talk to educators who are caught in the grind of turnaround efforts, they almost always express frustration about the short tenure of the turnaround principal.

The high turnover rate of turnaround principals will never permit sustained improvements. Therefore, school districts must be committed to hiring and selecting a "true" turnaround principal—and not simply a principal with a good track record of improving *non*-turnaround schools. A principal who has performed well at average schools will not necessarily have the traits needed to improve turnaround schools. These schools need leaders who are well informed of their challenges and who have the critical consciousness and social justice focus that allow them to deeply connect with students and get students engaged with their own education.

To understand the needs of principals and the dynamics of persistently failing schools, it is vital to listen to the stories of turnaround principals who have served in the trenches. This chapter presents the narratives of three critically conscious turnaround principals. The principals improved their chronically failing schools within one to two years and share the unique qualities of critically conscious turnaround principals.

The findings suggest that critically conscious turnaround principals were nurturing and passionate and felt a spiritual connection to lead their turnaround school toward academic achievement for all students. They knew the significance of critically conscious personnel, parent engagement, and building genuine relationships with students, parents, and the community. The findings align to the frameworks of critical theory and critical race theory.

This qualitative study was embarked upon to bring to light the lived experiences of principals who sought to eradicate oppressive school cultures in predominantly African American turnaround schools. The intent was to listen to the stories of lived experiences and capture an in-depth understanding of their transformative and social justice leadership that ultimately alleviated racial injustices.

This is not the first study of this type. George Theoharis in 2010 explored the disruption of injustice by six principals (two elementary, two middle, and two high school), which he characterized as an attempt at "breaking the silence" on the turnaround experience up close (Fine 1994, as cited in Theoharis 2010). Until then there had been little written about these principals. The "breaking the silence" approach was pivotal for Theoharis's qualitative study, because the existing literature often disparaged social justice leaders who did not fit the traditional mold, and their approaches were usually not accepted by colleagues and norms (Dantley 2002; Rapp 2002; Theoharis 2007).

Theoharis (2010) found that the efforts to create more just and equitable schools became exhausting for the principals. His report detailed various types of resistance and barriers from within the school and community and from the district and beyond—such resistance described as enormous, unceasing, and often unbearable. Theoharis used a purposeful and snowballing sampling approach.

The principals identified four kinds of injustice and used the following strategies to disrupt injustice: (1) eliminating school structures that marginalize, segregate, and impede achievement; (2) deprofessionalizing teaching staff; (3) enhancing school climates that needed to be more welcoming to marginalized families and building bridges between school and community, low-income families, and families of color; and (4) stepping up all efforts to combat disparate and low student achievement.

A series of lessons were learned, but more importantly, the social justice leaders provided a model of what can happen in schools for marginalized students. The model emphasizes the need to be relentless and grounded in social justice—not in merely theoretical terms but in actual schools with real-life leaders. Each of Theoharis's principals confronted different challenges and took slightly different approaches to create a more socially just school.

But they all shared a common theme: maintaining structures that isolate, track, and segregate instead of fostering inclusion and belonging of all kinds that will continue to oppress marginalized students; disrupting those structures is crucial. Inclusion is a moral issue in schools. As social justice leaders, principals must collaboratively plan differentiated curricula and programs of instruction that can meet all student needs when carried out in a warm and welcoming school and classroom setting.

They must create school communities that trust and empower the staff. These social justice principals held onto the idealism that social justice in schools is a necessary ongoing struggle, but they "broke the silence" and disrupted injustice while bringing life to social justice leadership (Theoharis 2010). In the study of turnaround principals who sought to eradicate oppressive school cultures in predominantly African American turnaround schools, similar findings resulted in the same drive and determination.

THE IMPORTANCE OF CRITICALLY CONSCIOUS TURNAROUND PRINCIPALS

For the study, in-depth interviews with three turnaround principals were the form of data collection. Table 5.1 shares descriptions of the turnaround principals along with details of the failing schools in which they worked.

Dr. Jim is an African American male in the Deep South who has been a principal in two different turnaround schools. Previously, he turned around a high school, taking the school from an F performance grade to a B performance grade in four years—a metric that some districts use to assign "performance grades" and keep schools accountable. Dr. Jim improved the graduation rate from 65 percent to 89 percent. His current school, he has raised the performance grade of an F school to a C school. Though

Table 5.1 Participant Demographics

Participant name	Region of United States	Age range	Years as educator	Years in educational leadership	Level of education	Years as turnaround principal
Dr. Jim	Deep South	45–50	23	11	PhD	10.5
Mrs. Tonya	Southeast	45–50	22	8	Master's	2
Dr. Benjamin	Southeast	45–50	23	16	PhD	8

improvements happened, Dr. Jim endured negative media attention for attempting to transform the school.

A small group of white teachers held meetings intended to turn students against the administration with misleading, negative information about the principal and school administration. After those schemes did not work, the same teachers went to the teachers' union to complain that Dr. Jim was leading the school with fear. Despite the negative attention, Dr. Jim remains at the school and making great strides with leading the school without the presence of specific teachers. The student population for his current school is 95 percent African American, 3 percent Hispanic, and about 2 percent white.

Mrs. Tonya is an African American female in the Southeast with the fewest number of years leading a turnaround school among the participants. The school had chronically failed students since 1997 while under the leadership of one principal, until the arrival of Mrs. Tonya in the summer of 2018. In one year, the drastic improvements by way of school leadership moved the school from a performance grade of an F to a C. Mrs. Tonya received media attention, but of a far different type than Dr. Jim.

One local newspaper called her efforts "Operation Save the School" and called the transformation an opportunity for the school's "epic future." She also received media attention for opening the school's first food pantry for the school community, as she recognized that students learn better when they're adequately fed nutrition for developmental needs. The student population at her school is 87 percent African American, 5 percent Hispanic, and 8 percent white.

Dr. Benjamin is an African American male in the Southeast who has led the turnaround school the longest number of years among the participants. Based on his transformative leadership, he has turned the school around from a performance grade of an F to a C+. His leadership led the school to the highest graduation rate in the school district. The media response to his efforts was focused on celebrating the 30-point graduation rate increase and students receiving $5.2 million in college scholarships. The student population is 72 percent African American, 21 percent Hispanic, and 6 percent Asian, biracial, or white.

Interviews served as the sole form of data collection. Due to participants residing in the Southeastern and Deep South region of the country, teleconferences and telephone interviews were used for data collection. Each participant was interviewed one time with an unscripted timeframe. For narrative inquiry and one-on-one situations, participants told their stories in a variety of ways: by responding to more or less structured interview questions or by engaging in conversation or dialogue (Clandinin 2013).

The goal of narrative interviewing is to generate detailed accounts rather than brief answers or general statements (Riessman 2008). Therefore, both in-depth and semi-structured interviews were conducted, as interviews provided unique insights into the complex lives of individuals (Kim 2015). Data collection, data analysis, and report writing are not distinct steps in the process—they are interrelated and often go on simultaneously in a research project (Creswell and Poth 2018).

The interview themes were coded by identifying words or short phrases that correlated with certain themes or ideas. Inductive coding was used to analyze the raw textual data by reading and interpreting it to develop concepts, themes, or a process model (Thomas 2006; Boyatzis 1998; Corbin and Strauss 1990). An examination of the relationships among similar codes was combined to create a category (Kim 2015). Each principal led a turnaround school in a different state.

Despite these differences, seven themes surfaced from the coding process: (1) the spiritual calling to accept the challenge of school turnaround; (2) the disruption and eradication of systemic and institutional racism; (3) the removal of deficit thinking and oppressive mindsets of teachers; (4) the deliberate miseducation of students; (5) the drastic reduction of suspensions to remove racial inequity; (6) purposeful professional development to meet teachers' needs; and (7) the need for experiential preparation programs to educate critically conscious principals. Table 5.2 lists the themes derived from an analysis of the participants' in-depth and semi-structured interviews.

Table 5.2 Themes from In-Depth and Semi-structured Interviews

Theme 1	Spiritual calling to accept challenge of school turnaround
Theme 2	Disruption and eradication of systemic and institutional racism
Theme 3	Removal of deficit thinking and oppressive mindsets of teachers
Theme 4	Deliberate miseducation of students
Theme 5	Drastic reduction of suspensions to remove racial inequity
Theme 6	Purposeful professional development to meet teachers' needs
Theme 7	Experiential preparation programs educating critically conscious principals

Theme 1: The Spiritual Calling to Accept the Challenge of School Turnaround

To accept the challenge of school turnaround, it's necessary to have leaders who are passionate and dedicated to transforming a persistently low turnaround school into a thriving school that's advancing children academically. Two of the three participants voiced a connection to leading a turnaround school as a spiritual calling for school turnaround work. While listening to the participants, a clear connection was evident among the critically conscious leaders who used the source of motivation from their spiritual identities to serve as civil rights activists or organic intellectuals who not only articulate an agenda for the radical reconstruction of schools but also actually implement a social justice agenda (Dantley 2010).

All of the participants expressed the value of supporting the needs of students, teachers, and families within their school communities as they believed that students are worthy of a dynamic leader who seeks students' true potential and refuses to accept that students were not capable of succeeding academically. Mrs. Tonya shared how her appointment to the turnaround school evolved:

> Being here, it's God's grace. Being a principal over here is night and day [from] the experiences I bring from a non–Title I [nonturnaround school] experience... It's like a calling. (Personal communication, February 20 2020)

Similarly, Dr. Benjamin believed in his spiritual calling to become the principal of the turnaround school. He was asked to lead the turnaround school five times before finally accepting God's calling. He realized that allowing another principal to take the helm was a risk that he was unwilling to take:

> [It was] not going be fair to those kids, for somebody who didn't know anything about this building, they know nothing about this community, they know nothing about these children . . . to come in here and then there's this expectation that you fix it. I say it's not fair to the kids. It's not fair to faculty. It's not fair to the community, because there's going be somebody else who is going stay one or two years and what they need is continuity in the leadership. (Personal communication, March 5 2020)

Dr. Benjamin drove past his current school multiple times before taking on the principalship. He remembers these early encounters:

> As driving to take the Praxis . . . it fell on my spirit that "You're going to be right there." Didn't know anything about this school, didn't know anything

about the community, didn't know anything about the school's history, none of it. But something said this is where you're going to be. Time and again passing the school, it fell on my spirit: "That's where you're going be."

Fast-forward to the end of the year . . . Things just did not work out in my current school. Me and the principal fell out over some of the things that I saw happening specifically to black kids. We parted ways and my résumé was out and the principal called me to interview me on the phone for about forty-five to fifty minutes . . . a really honest conversation, and she said, "I want you to meet the team."

She gave me the address of the school and when coming down the street and making the turn . . . almost broke down in tears because God told me this is where you're going to be and this is the school. (Personal communication, March 5, 2020)

Furthermore, Dr. Benjamin praises God continuously, saying, "Thank God . . . still in love with the work and enjoying it . . . still like the challenge of it. To me that's the rewarding part . . . you actually get to see yourself make a difference" (Personal communication, March 5, 2020). Both Dr. Benjamin and Mrs. Tonya were clearly transformative educational leaders who were grounded in African American spirituality, and that spiritual base was crucial for the dismantling and constructing of a different reality for students, one based in equity and social justice (Dantley 2010).

Theme 2: The Disruption and Eradication of Systemic and Institutional Racism

A critical analysis of exactly how racism impacted the turnaround principals' leadership was vital. Two out of the three participants, Dr. Jim and Mrs. Tonya, felt that the resistance of improvement efforts to change the schools was rooted in systemic racism. Systemic racism is how ideas of white superiority are captured in everyday thinking at a systems level and taking in the big picture of how society operates, rather than looking at one-on-one interactions (O'Dowd 2020).

This type of institutional racism operates from established and respected forces in society and thus receives far less public condemnation (Gillborn 2008). Atkins and Oglesby (2019) recognized that racism is about systems that marginalize people of color. Theoharis (2009) referenced how the seven principals understood the need to push forward ongoing efforts around race in order to foster changes in attitudes and behavior that consciously or unconsciously contributed to white privilege in their schools.

Taylor (2009) noted that white superiority is so ingrained in political, legal, and educational structures that they are almost unrecognizable (as cited in

Pitre, Allen, and Pitre 2015) but a critically conscious leader recognizes these structures. Dr. Jim's heart-wrenching experiences when attempting to disrupt and eradicate systemic racism were alarming. He described an immunization effort by the school district that seemed experimental, at least when it came to his school:

> At one point the district wanted to have African American students immunized. But instead of taking a shot or immunization, they wanted to come in and put something in the students' noses. I completely went against that notion. We were the only school that it would have been taking place at . . . that was something that was not happening at any white schools or any other schools and it was not going happen at our school either. My thoughts where they wanted to try something at a poor school while not many people would catch it and we didn't allow it to happen. (Personal communication, February 24, 2020)

Next, Mrs. Tonya's experience stepped into the political realm for how her state's senators changed an education bill that directly impacted turnaround schools without listening to the voices of educators who were doing the tireless work of leading turnaround schools. She shared the details of a senate committee meeting where she voiced her concerns to not discontinue the funding of turnaround schools with the most marginalized communities:

> We need extra funding, because what happens is when you take the funding away, that is people that can provide interventions for kids. Forty percent of the kindergartners have never been at school; they arrive to the school two years behind and it takes time to fix that. But it also takes people; when the funding is taken away, who's supposed to fix that? They're holding us to the same standards as everybody else but we have a different set of barriers that schools can't change.
>
> Schools are in a really bad situation and politicians are purposefully trying to take over public schools to turn them into charters because they want to make money. Trying to advocate for our schools and for our teachers and for our kids is a hard thing to do when it feels like you're talking to a group of white people who have never taught in a school and don't even know what this is like . . . trying to explain . . . but it made no difference . . . it's like you're speaking on deaf ears. (Personal communication February 20, 2020)

When asking Mrs. Tonya, "Do you think this [discontinuing of funding] is based on the ethnicity of the schools?" she responded, "I do. I would like to not believe that, but that's the way it felt with every senator that was present at that meeting. They were white and I only know of one that was a former educator and he was never in a Title 1 school. I could be wrong, hope I'm wrong, but I feel like it is" (Personal communication, February 20, 2020).

Dr. Benjamin's experience was somewhat different; as the principal of a largely African American staff, he was challenged by same-race teachers attempting to maintain the status quo. He identified African American teachers as gatekeepers to African American students' equitable education, but his school was still plagued by the effects of long-term struggles:

Being at a historically black high school with a legacy . . . it was not largely about race. It's usually about low expectations from quite a few black educators, and that was what was disappointing. That first year in 2012, and by the end of the school year, we had to fill forty-two vacancies over the summer, everything from administration down to the custodians.

What I observed was this indifference about the school but, more importantly, an indifference about the kids. Stuff was done with no intention, no intentional or expected outcomes; sometimes there were not even lesson plans. (Personal communication, March 5, 2020)

What Dr. Benjamin found was that the teachers had absorbed the hopelessness and lack of belief in the students' potential from the greater culture. It is a process known as *dysconscious racism*, in which people in the oppressed group assimilate the dominant narrative of white norms and privilege (King 1991). King devised this term to facilitate college students' recognition of their own miseducation that contributes to the unequal educational outcomes of students and leads to the teachers' reinforcement of societal inequities and oppression (ibid.).

This is compounded by the multigenerational trauma of the African American community that continues to suffer the effects of centuries of slavery, oppression, and the experiences of institutionalized racism of today (Degruy [2005] 2017). Degruy called this Post Traumatic Slave Syndrome. The influence of dysconscious racism and the trauma of centuries of oppression causes some African American teachers to fall short in uplifting and empowering African American students.

The African American teachers in Dr. Benjamin's school had low expectations for themselves and the students, and the lack of love for themselves and their students diminished their African American students' potential (Degruy [2005] 2017). The African American teachers lacked a critical consciousness of their own experience and of white culture and privilege, therefore unconsciously sustaining institutionalized and structural racism in the school. The teachers' story shows that when systemic injustices remain unspoken or accepted, an unethical white privilege is fostered. But when individuals and groups point out systemic injustices and inequities, the dominant culture is made accountable (O'Dowd 2020).

Theme 3: Removal of Deficit Thinking and the Oppressive Mindsets of Teachers

When trying to analyze how critically conscious turnaround principals address inequity and oppression in schools or deal with teachers who demonstrate an oppressive mentality, the themes that surfaced were eye-opening. All three of the critically conscious turnaround principals stepped into the turnaround roles by addressing deficit thinking and the oppressive mindsets of teachers. All three principals knew that changing the mindset of teachers was a non-negotiable in order to meet the needs of the students.

Theoharis (2009) grasped that social justice leaders highlight their leadership on issues of equity and justice; therefore, they lead with an intentional transformation to create schools that oppose oppression and suffering through transforming schools into models of equity and communities of justice. Dr. Benjamin explained how he needed to address the mindset of the entire school community when it came to intentional transformation:

> We need to do the right thing, making sure we do the right thing by the teachers, the students, the parents, the community. Most times my thoughts are people think kids aren't deserving of the extra effort, a certain caliber of kid, a certain kind of kid, kids coming from certain neighborhoods, they're not deserving of the time, the patience, the commitment, the dedication that's required to literally turn a school around and move it in the right direction. (Personal communication, March 5, 2020)

When asked about the population of students within the school and whether this had anything to do with people thinking this way, Dr. Benjamin responded:

> Just being here, having visited other turnaround schools and having talked to the turnaround principals who have been successful, that's the common theme. People think these children are expendable. You'll always find out who people are because everybody tells you they love kids until they have to work with them every day.
>
> You think it's just about the academic part only to find out that it's greater. Then you're still responsible for the academic part, but also dealing with the emotional part, the mental part . . . how do you build a child that may not have the same morals and values as you, if they have or if they even understand the

concept of morals and values? It's all those things you have to attend to in a turnaround school. In the past these things have just been left unaddressed . . . no accountability. (Personal communication, March 5, 2020)

Sometimes the mindset was not just a passive failure but an active attempt to perpetuate myths about different student populations. Dr. Benjamin spoke about a teacher who had a child of her own in a prominent white school in a neighboring school district. He noticed this teacher was perpetuating myths about the school, citing a brawl between the turnaround school's basketball team and another school: "This teacher didn't see what happened . . . the expectations of the kids that she's responsible for teaching . . . and now you got to go . . . already started the process of recommending that her contract not be renewed, but that incident helped to accelerate the process" (Personal communication, March 5, 2020).

Dr. Benjamin believed this incident was not necessarily about race because he noticed African American teachers holding the same deficit thinking toward students in the turnaround school, a fact that Carter Woodson himself noted back in the early twentieth century (Woodson [1933] 2018). Dr. Benjamin explained:

Some people were very negative, condescending. And these were black people. So, I tell people all the time, our first job is always to look for the best educator possible. I know you want a school full of black teachers. No, that's not the driving force for me. I'm always looking for great teachers. If you are Black, Blue, Asian, Purple, White, that doesn't matter to me. I just want to make sure that you're a great teacher and you're a great fit for our school and you want to see our students do well. That's it. (Personal communication, March 5, 2020)

Dr. Jim and Mrs. Tonya had similar experiences with the deficit thinking of teachers in their turnaround school setting. Tonya's lived experience was more alarming because teachers were victims of deficit thinking toward themselves due to the previous principal's nineteen years of applying the "banking concept to encourage passivity in the oppressed" (Freire [1970] 2000). The teachers' lack of critical consciousness hindered the achievement of students for a number of years. Therefore, Mrs. Tonya acted swiftly to transform the school for the welfare of the students because the teachers were in a detrimental state:

These teachers were oppressed, for lack of a better word . . . I'm still kind of struggling with it today. They were given two folders a day. One was a math folder, and one was a language arts folder, and in each folder there were worksheets. And their job every morning was to make sure that the worksheets were finished and returned by the end of the day. My question was, what happens when you don't turn it in? And they said, "Oh, you wouldn't dare find out. You turned them in."

And what would happen is, the office staff would stamp them with smiley faces and stars and then return them to the kids. But they weren't checking them for correctness; it was just a task that people were doing. So these teachers were putting all of their energy into these worksheets, and they were not groomed for proper teaching and learning to take place. (Personal communication, February 20, 2020)

Mrs. Tonya was dedicated to changing the school culture because she understood that the shortfall of the teachers' mindsets would ultimately affect the instruction that the students received. She explained:

Telling teachers and giving them autonomy to teach was difficult, because they'd say, "Well, no, you just tell me what to do." I would give them some choices, and they'd say, "Whatever you think is best." I wanted to change that. (Personal communication, February 20, 2020)

As for Dr. Jim, his experience was similar to Dr. Benjamin's in the sense that there were teachers in the turnaround school with deficit thinking regarding the students and it was critical to remove those teachers from the school setting. As Dr. Jim explained, "Some of the challenges were seeing that teachers were orchestrating themes that kind of put the students against the administration. Going through some of the sessions they were having with the students, I noted those things. It was just a matter of moving those teachers out." (Personal communication, February 24, 2020)

Theme 4: The Deliberate Miseducation of Students

Carter Woodson taught long ago about the miseducation of African American students, but his lessons are still pertinent today. The idea of the inferiority of African American students is drilled into them in almost every class and every book they study. Because of this, critically conscious principals must be centrally concerned about advancing inclusion, access, and opportunity (Theoharis 2009).

But trying to advance inclusion will be insufficient if the curriculum is inadequate and the teachers do not have the will or skills to reach each student. The three principals steered efforts to dismantle the miseducation of students, specifically African Americans. With a national teaching force that is nearly 90 percent white, school leaders need to address the crisis of cultural incongruence (Pitre, Allen, and Pitre 2015) and the impacts of damaging pedagogy that happens so often in turnaround schools.

Dr. Jim explained his experience of cultural incongruence:

> [There was a] culture and a climate created by the white teachers who were pretty much running the school, and they were setting low expectations. They had run off the last three principals, three in a row, and I was to be the fourth, I guess. So my biggest challenge was dismantling this effort and being a social justice advocate.
>
> I realized they had low expectations for students and they actually were pitting the students against me and the administration. We had to really dismantle that effort and go up against the teachers' union. It was a big battle to actually attempt and try to change the way things were going here at the school. (Personal communication, February 24, 2020)

Kunjufu (2006) explained that the future of African Americans is "in the hands of white female teachers" (11). Because of this, achievement may not be accessible to African American students the way it is for white students, regardless of economics, involvement, or attitudes (Atkins and Oglesby 2019). Still, Sleeter (2012) stated that teachers in schools where students are underachieving tend to be pressured by principals and districts toward standardization rather than responsiveness to their diverse students. Students in turnaround schools often endure a magnitude of harmful pedagogy, but critically conscious principals can rectify the miseducation of African American students.

Mrs. Tonya's experience of miseducation in her school was particularly wrenching because she led an elementary school—and elementary students' brain is still developing and absorption of knowledge is critical. The National Dropout Prevention Center states that birth-to-five interventions and providing enriching activities and enriching environments in early childhood can enhance brain development (National Dropout Prevention Center 2021).

It's no coincidence that the dropout rate of students begins in elementary school, not in high school. In elementary schools, many times, the principal and teacher hold end-of-the-year meetings to discuss students' performance rates. Retention and promotion of students are discussed to determine which students will be promoted and which will be held back in the same grade level. Even though some students may benefit from retention to grasp foundational skills needed for the next grade level, there may be resistance from parents, teachers, and/or principals in which an elementary child continues to transition from one grade level to the next.

As educators, the inherited term is *social promotion*—promoting a student from one grade to the next based on their age and the developmental advances of the student in comparison with their peers. Social promotion typically takes place in elementary school and sometimes in middle school. Yet, once students transition from middle school to high school, social promotion is null and void since high school graduation requirements/credits are involved and the student must pass a specific course to move to the next grade level.

Unfortunately, if the student endured social promotion for a number of years in elementary or middle school and possibly fell through the cracks as some educators' reference, then many students lack critical foundational skills which will limit their ability to grasp high school content. This is the grim reality with many high school students who struggle in the high school setting, which contributes to the high school dropout in ninth or tenth grade, the influx of freshman academies in the early 2000s to capture many ninth graders from failing, and the school-to-prison pipeline.

Students who are disconnected with learning and school become frustrated and discouraged. At times, students' behaviors may display the frustration of the student, for example, many students who were socially promoted are possibly reading on an elementary or middle school level while attending high school. Thus, providing the best possible classroom environment from the early childhood years throughout secondary years is the most effective way to reduce the number of children who will ultimately drop out of school (National Dropout Prevention Center 2020). Mrs. Tonya shared the dismal experience of a fifth grader:

> Many kids were promoted to the next grade without having proven themselves worthy. It just seemed like there was no rhyme or reason to it. If this kid was making consistent F's and D's, they moved on—and I'm talking about between kindergarten and second grade. Those kids matriculate through every grade level and then they become a fourth grader and that's when people realize, "Oh, he might have a learning disability," or "We have a fifth grader right now that could not sound out the word *church* six months ago because she missed foundational phonics in kindergarten and first grade."
>
> There were teachers here that clearly weren't teaching, and learning wasn't taking place. First grade is everything, but these first graders are now fifth graders, and many of them cannot read. It's not a fault of their own; it's because they went through every grade level and didn't get the proper intervention early on. (Personal communication, February 20, 2020)

Fortunately, with Mrs. Tonya's critically conscious and social justice leadership, she helped these students who suffered in their primary grades, which are "shining stars" now and made drastic academic gains (Personal communication, February 20, 2020). She entered the turnaround school realizing that removing deficit thinking of teachers was a priority. Teachers were victims of deficit thinking toward themselves because the previous principal, who led the school for nineteen years, led the school with the "banking concept" that discouraged creative thinking and critical exploration.

The first agenda item for Mrs. Tonya was to develop her teachers in order for the teachers to believe in their gifts to teach children. She immediately put an end to the daily worksheet routine, and she worked to develop her teachers into effective teachers with critical pedagogy skills. Implicit or explicit, biases surface in many classrooms, which contribute to the failure of some teachers to respond with cultural appropriateness to the needs of African American students.

The beliefs and actions of some teachers result in a lack of culturally relevant instruction for African American students. Ladson-Billings (Ladson-Billings and Tate 1995) identified the need for learning to be "culturally relevant" and argued for its centrality in the academic success of African American and other children. Schools that implement a multicultural education challenge and reject racism and other forms of discrimination affirm the pluralism that students, their communities, and teachers reflect (Pitre 2014).

The miseducation of African American students happens on many levels. Dr. Benjamin noticed that African American students were not exposed to scholarship, summer, and career opportunities that could help them continue their education:

> Scholarship opportunities . . . only a certain group of people got that information, whether it was intentional or not, so I decided to give everybody an e-mail account and all of the students had an e-mail address. My expectation was that you read your emails once a day. That way, everyone got the same notices about scholarships and so on. (Personal communication, March 5, 2020)

The miseducation of students is damaging based on short-term and long-term outcomes. Libassi stated that the United States fails to incorporate African American and Hispanic people into many key professions, like engineering and education. The inclusion of these bright minds from these professions would improve the economic prospects of thousands of African American and Hispanic families. Their exclusion will create a long-term competitive disadvantage for the United States, as the next great scientific breakthrough or great tech endeavor may be left undiscovered by a student whose potential was disregarded (Libassi 2018).

Clearly, all of the participants in the study recognized the need to remedy this issue. Therefore, they worked attentively to plan differentiated curriculum and instruction to meet all student needs in a warm and welcoming school and classroom, along with creating school communities that are trusting and empowering to the staff (Theoharis 2010).

Theme 5: The Drastic Reduction of Suspensions to Remove Racial Inequity

There is a mass amount of literature demonstrating a racial bias when it comes to removing students from the educational setting based on disciplinary practices, including suspensions and expulsions. Recognizing and eradicating the inequitable punitive measures against African American students is the first step in a long, terrible journey. Studies show that children of color are consistently overrepresented at every point of the school-to-prison pipeline (Kim et al. 2010).

From 1973 to 2006, the percentage of African American students enrolled in public schools who were suspended at least once in a given year rose from 6 percent to 15 percent, and those racial disparities carry over into arrests and referrals into the juvenile justice system (ibid.). The three principals in the study all recognized the immediate need to address the suspension rate of the turnaround school. Mrs. Tonya recognized this problem even on the elementary level:

> There were four hundred referrals for behavior [out of roughly 1300 students] that equaled hours of lost instruction. So, one of our main goals was keeping kids at school and handling the consequences here instead of sending them home. We came up with our behavior plan, which kept the kids at school. Under this plan, we might still have removed them from the classroom in the situation, but at least learning continued to take place in another classroom setting . . . we went from four hundred suspensions to ninety last year. So we have a system in place that kind of gives kids a second chance. (Personal communication, February 20, 2020)

Dr. Benjamin and Dr. Jim observed similar issues in their high schools and knew they needed to act quickly to remove the racial inequities of suspending African American students. Dr. Benjamin was startled when analyzing his suspension data:

> When I first got here, our suspension rate was almost 25 percent and they didn't have a principal, so APs just did what they knew . . . just suspend kids. You think about all of those days of no instruction . . . that was clearly one of the first things we had to get a grip on. A lot of the suspensions were over very frivolous kinds of things, such as students playing around too rough in the hallway and disregarding teachers' redirection, or two students cursing in the room after the teacher attempted to redirect their language.
>
> Some of the behavior referrals could have been addressed by the teacher instead of elevating the issue to the school administration; this is classroom management 101. Our plan was really about giving students a voice—you

know, talk to us; how can we better meet your needs? Now we're looking at a suspension rate of 4 percent or 3 percent.

It was largely about building relationships, bridging relationships with students, bridging relationships with families. We have a restorative practices coordinator now who does restorative circles with students. This is not just when things go wrong but even when the class is just kind of off. A teacher can request for the restorative practices coordinator to come and do a restorative circle with students and adults. (Personal communication, March 5, 2020)

Dr. Jim also had to tackle the disproportionate suspension rate. He started by "having teachers that are prepared to deal with students from high-poverty areas, looking at policies and procedures that are in place to minimize how students are treated or how consequences are given out, making sure our staff are more culturally competent as it relates to the students. Now the suspensions are down" (Personal communication, February 24, 2020). Dr. Jim gathered his leadership team to begin analyzing and discussing the suspension data of the school.

Next, he began changing the protocols for behavior referrals; he wanted to support the teachers but also help clarify which behavior infractions required a behavior referral and which infractions did not. Lastly, he provided his teachers professional development on multicultural education so they would become more culturally competent and equipped to educate students whose upbringing may have been different from their own upbringing. Addressing the substantial racial inequity in suspensions and other punitive measures helped these principals create a school culture detached from the systemic racial discriminations that many African American students undergo in schools.

Alternative discipline may include restorative circles to restore the school community with building relationships and restoring the harm that has been done, create a special room for in-school suspension for a short period of time and deliver behavior interventions and instruction to students, incorporate social–emotional learning skills and character traits that help students improve behaviors. Any of these practices can be combined with strategies like collaborative problem-solving and conflict circles to offer teachers a wide array of approaches that focus on the students' need for expressing themselves and learning positive coping mechanisms.

Theme 6: Purposeful Professional Development to Meet Teachers' Needs

The turnaround principals interviewed had a combined experience of sixty-eight years in education, starting in the classroom. The experience as a teacher helped the turnaround principal understand the importance of developing teachers in a way that will allow them to inspire and hold high expectations for the students whom they served. In each school, a focus to shift the culture of the school and cater to the needs of teachers through professional development or the use of teacher/instructional coaches was imperative.

There was an awareness of the cultural incongruence with having white teachers in a school with predominantly African American students. Yet, each principal believed that this imbalance could be reconciled when white educators are trained to be culturally responsive teachers and to incorporate the cultural experiences of students into their pedagogy (Ladson-Billings 2009, as cited in Pitre, Hudson, Smith-Gray, and Carrington James 2020). Mrs. Tonya explained how she addresses professional development:

> The school became an F, I think, for a multitude of reasons, but how the previous principal managed teachers was a part of it. I think that one of my gifts is being able to coach teachers, to give teachers the tools to teach, guide them through it, and provide professional development. Now everybody has what they need to be the best that they can be. They just didn't know the proper route to get there.
>
> I believe if you take care of the teachers, everything else works. A lot of people say it's all about the kids, but here it's about the teachers. I do my best to raise money to be able to spoil and do things for them. And when they're happy and happy about being here, they will do anything it takes to make all these plans I have work for the students. (Personal communication, February 20, 2020)

Dr. Jim believed in developing his teachers by utilizing instructional coaches and other conscious leaders. "Facilitating the growth of the staff is really training my assistants and my instructional leaders. I have them train twenty or twenty-five teachers with two instructional coaches and another administrator, then have them work with the teachers for teacher development" (Personal communication, February 24, 2020).

Dr. Benjamin also expressed that teacher development was important. He realized the crucial importance of "attending to their professional development needs and doing meaningful professional development at the school level. Clearly, we can't send everybody out or always hire somebody to come in, but teachers expressed an interest in leadership, helping to develop their leadership potential and giving them an opportunity to serve in formal leadership roles" (Personal communication, March 5, 2020). Part of this process was disrupting harmful racial mindsets by purposefully developing his teaching staff. He would circulate articles on racial bias and foster discussions around the articles:

> Our last article came from this *IB World* magazine titled "Racial Bias in Education: Breaking the Glass Ceiling to Opportunity." And that was our focus: how racial bias presents itself, how we might be perpetuating these things unbeknownst to us, and being mindful. It's kind of like the whole idea of microaggressions.
>
> I need to bring it to the faculty's attention and then help them to be able to create spaces where people feel comfortable saying, "Hey, this is what just happened and I need you to correct it," or "How do we move forward from this experience?" I think people often don't know that's what they're doing; it's unconscious.
>
> At the last faculty meeting, I had everybody do the racial bias test through Harvard. Everybody had to bring their results, but I didn't make them share their results unless they wanted to. But we had these white teachers that would say, "My tests show that I have a strong preference for Black people," which seemed unlikely. So I had to have hard conversations. I'm working with the teachers about racial biases in how we treat people, how their behavior or attitude might come off.
>
> A teacher might not see it as a matter of race, but based on people's experiences, that's how it can feel. Especially children—Black children. You may think you're just being matter of fact or getting straight to the point, but that's not how people are internalizing their experience with you. They're seeing you as mean, callous, resentful, condescending, or racist, and their perception is their reality. You've got to help them deal with that because you helped foster that in their minds. You have to have those genuine real conversations with people. (Personal communication, March 5, 2020)

These principals have learned what Theoharis and Haddix (2011) found in their study on successful principals of students of color. These principals did not avoid racial issues but talked about race with their staff "plainly and often."

Theme 7: Experiential Preparation Programs Educating Critically Conscious Principals

A final theme that emerged from the study was the need for universities to adequately prepare current and future turnaround principals. Pitre (2015) noted that colleges of education will have to play a vital role to ensure that a multicultural education is part of every K-12 school. Two of the three critically conscious turnaround principals discussed their preparation programs as it relates to transformative and social justice leadership; the third participant did not attend an experiential preparation program and learned his leadership skills smack in the midst of the turbulent turnaround school.

Addressing the persistent racial issues in America's schools must begin with the universities and colleges that prepare and train teachers and educational leaders. Universities and colleges should prepare the predominantly white teacher population for the diverse student population that will be in their schools and classrooms. The growing number of students of diverse racial, ethnic, class, and language backgrounds in U.S. schools became an issue for many white teacher candidates who had little experience in multicultural school and societal settings.

The overwhelmingly white teaching force has little preparation to deal with demographic changes now underway or training to teach their students about the contributions and cultures of other groups in the society (Frankenberg and Siegel-Hawley 2008). Two principals in the study attended an experiential preparation in the Deep South. Both received a thorough understanding of social justice leadership by observing and listening to local principals of struggling schools in the region. Ladson-Billings (2000) argued that preparation programs should assign field experiences to teacher candidates who would possibly play a role in addressing the stereotypes and racist attitudes that teachers may hold.

Dr. Jim's master's program helped graduate students understand the realities of current-day schools. The university scheduled speakers from local schools and communities to visit classes on a weekly basis, reporting on the critical issues the schools faced (Personal communication, February 24, 2020). The coursework for his doctorate also included literature from distinguished scholars such as Jawanza Kunjufu, Sonia Nieto, Chance Lewis, Gloria Ladson-Billings, and Geneva Gay.

These scholars offer deep insights into the miseducation of African American children, the importance of social justice in education, multicultural education, teacher education, and the education of students of culturally and linguistically diverse backgrounds. Dr. Jim's doctoral program encouraged the students to critique distinguished authors' literature on educating African American children. As a result, the university prepared educators to analyze the current-day obstacles of African American children and develop into a critically conscious individual. Dr. Jim's personal doctoral work centered on the overrepresentation of African American male students in special education.

Dr. Benjamin's preparation program also helped him to become critically conscious of the racial inequities of today's schools:

> The professors had you going into the field and actually kind of doing a comparative analysis of one school district that's in a prominent area versus another school district that's in an impoverished area. We clearly saw these inequities, and our focus was on coming up with a proposal to address them. The inequity was, of course, in the funding because it was a school finance course. And we searched for ways to reduce these funding inequities. (Personal communication, March 5, 2020)

Ladson-Billings (2000) recognized how teacher preparation programs should assign students with field experiences that help them overcome any stereotypes and racist attitudes that they may have as a future educator. Currently, Dr. Benjamin works in the Southeast, but his preparation program was in the Deep South, and the field experiences in local schools helped him become the critically conscious leader that he is now:

> [Many African Americans] inherently think white people know a lot and they're smart until you're in those classes and you realize, "Oh, oh . . . okay, really ya'll don't know." It was an eye-opening experience. Having gone to high school, elementary, middle school, in mostly predominately black schools where I did fairly well academically, I was still aware of how white supremacy is really ingrained in our heads.
> Like, you know, you're not going to be able to compete against white people. My mom used to always tell me, "Remember your best is just good to them." So you take all that with you into these classrooms and then you realize that "Oh . . . the lack of consciousness." (Personal communication, March 5, 2020)

Mrs. Tonya's preparation program fell short in the area of developing pre-service educators to hold a critical consciousness through field experiences or in-depth reading about social justice education. She said, "there was not any textbook or book that I read that shaped how I lead" (Personal communication, February 20, 2020). This is the case with many preparation programs. There is a dire need to educate all students, which means preparing leaders to be critically conscious social justice change agents in chronically failing schools.

CONCLUSION

Addressing the need for exceptional, critically conscious turnaround principals may very well be the solution to solving the epidemic of low-performing schools. But the average turnaround principal faces many challenges to abruptly change the trajectory of the school. At the same time, those same principals may face dismissal when overly traumatic changes to the school's culture and performance outcomes result in stagnation.

The qualitative study investigated how critically conscious principals thought about their work in turnaround schools and how they handled the challenges within the school community. Each principal shared their lived experiences as they embarked upon a chronically failing school and turned the low-performing school around. The necessary steps included addressing teachers who demonstrated oppressive mindsets, coming up with new behavior plans to reduce suspensions, and fostering open discussions about race among the staff.

The approach was sometimes aided by their own teacher preparation courses and sometimes not. Yet, all realized that universities must do a better job of preparing teachers and principals for the diverse and complicated schools that they will lead. No matter what the makeup of the school's teachers, transformative principals recognized the value of their teachers. They acknowledged the importance of competent, antiracist, and culturally responsive teachers to meet the needs of African American students.

They devised ways to make teachers feel safe and appreciated while also providing opportunities for teachers to learn about critical race issues. They also committed to staying with their schools long enough to see the transformation through and provide much-needed continuity. These leaders made the transformation of their schools a priority. Their results in raising their schools' graduation rates and performance grades are potent evidence of the importance of students being educated by critically conscious educators prepared to help marginlize students matriculate into today's society with confidence and dignity.

Chapter 6

Conclusion

Historically, underperforming schools present especially thorny turnaround challenges. Kowal and Hassel (2005) identified some of the structural reasons for this: (1) the multiple and external causes of underperformance, (2) the challenge of sustaining improved performance, and (3) the added complexity of attempting turnarounds on a large scale (Leithwood et al. 2010). The problems of turnaround schools have been evident since the 1960s.

Federal programs like No Child Left Behind and the SIG have struggled to make a difference for children at these schools, often ones with a large population of African American children and set in poor communities. Turnaround schools undergo high turnover rates for principals, and additional funding to transform these schools can exist one year and disappear the next. Old problems like high suspension rates for African American students and new ones like the burdens of standardized testing come into play.

Students are burdened with racism, overly adult responsibilities at home, and a myriad of mental health and physical health issues that impact their ability to learn. Teacher preparation courses at universities haven't fully prepared teachers for the realities of the twenty-first-century classroom and its diverse student body. Futhermore, federal programs with stringent requirements for metrics and reporting drove many talented principals and teachers from the profession.

But new ideas and strategies can still make a difference. In particular, the all-important role of the principal must be a focus like never before. Principals in turnaround schools have challenges like no others, and districts must be discerning regarding who they hire to lead these schools. One of the missing pieces of the puzzle of educating students in turnaround schools is to have principals who have a critical consciousness regarding race, ethnicity, and economics.

A critical consciousness encompasses an understanding of African American history (as well as the history of other disadvantaged groups, such as students with disabilities); insight into the current realities of students' everyday lives; and a powerful belief that all students deserve an equitable education and that all students can succeed. Such principals are determined to rectify the cycle of generational poverty and deliver their students the opportunities and growth that all students in our nation should have. This is a task that has life-altering consequences for their students' personal trajectories as well as the country's.

As a society, we believe knowledge is the gateway for success, whether students move on to college, the workforce, or entrepreneurship. Yet some students will transition from the educational system prepared for productive citizenship, while others will transition disoriented and ill-equipped to survive in today's society. At worst, students who are not prepared for success will be statistics for the nation's school-to-prison pipeline. The high cost of leaving these students unprepared and underdeveloped in terms of knowledge, experience, social skills, and higher education is one that the nation cannot afford. And one that marginalized students don't deserve to carry.

***

Only principals with a critical consciousness can begin to change this scenario. With an understanding of history, an awareness of students' current culture and community, and the ability to communicate this understanding to students and teachers alike, a turnaround principal can begin to tackle the factors that have built up a wall to students' success. Studies have demonstrated the concrete positive effects of such principals, and our qualitative study of three successful turnaround principals reinforced the truth of their impact.

Some factors are attitudinal, like a sense of pessimism about the school among the community and even teachers. After years of failure, there may be a latent belief that the cause is hopeless. Teachers may believe that the students are at fault or simply lack intelligence to succeed—a deficit mindset regarding their education that should be replaced with an understanding of an "education gap" rather than an "achievement gap." Other attitudinal factors are the understanding (or lack of understanding) of white supremacy and how it has contributed to the miseducation of Black students as well as the difference between equality and equity.

As Mrs. Tonya said of her school, "They're holding us to the same standards as everybody else but we have a different set of barriers that we can't change." The study's principals showed great creativity and wisdom in how they addressed these factors. One had open discussions with staff about race and even included readings that would illuminate the challenges of racism for some teachers who may not be aware of them. One acted to rid the staff of teachers who engaged in harmful stereotypes about the students in the turnaround school.

Others tried to educate teachers about implicit biases, microaggressions, cultural insensitivities, and racial discriminations, giving them insight into how students might perceive behaviors and attitude that, to the teachers, seem perfectly neutral. They worked to combat dysconscious racism, in which African American teachers have absorbed society's racist stereotypes of their students and become hopeless about their educational potential. Mrs. Tonya stepped into leadership at a school where teachers were provided with worksheets to hand out to students and collect at the end of the day.

The students' completed worksheets were given a sticker or smiley face but never evaluated for correctness, and students were certainly never taught to understand what they got wrong. The school had become a factory of the worst kind, with everyone keeping busy but no actual learning taking place. Mrs. Tonya eliminated the worksheets and worked hard to communicate the importance of actual instruction. She had to instill in the teachers a belief in their students and a belief in themselves. All of them worked to communicate a sense of possibility and positivity to both teachers and students.

There are also administrative factors to address. Two enormous challenges lay in transforming the punitive nature of discipline and revising the curriculum. A critically conscious principal will overhaul the entire disciplinary framework of the school. The racist over-discipline of African American students results in them being taken out of the classroom and having their instruction replaced by suspensions or expulsions.

To combat this loss of instructional time, some principals have enacted new behavior programs that train teachers to understand when they should send students out of the classroom and when the situation should be dealt with within the classroom. Dr. Benjamin established a restorative justice room where students were able to have a safe space to talk about their educational experiences with an adult; this provided an alternative to complete withdrawal from the learning environment via suspension or expulsion.

And they created new strategies for handling discipline with a restorative justice focus rather than a punitive focus. Those strategies included collaborative problem solving meetings between teachers and students, in which students were encouraged to talk about how they perceived their education and their place in the classroom, teachers listened attentively before sharing their own concerns, and they worked together on a solution that both of them felt they had agency in.

They included conflicts circles, in which students are invited to gather in a circle to do mindfulness exercises before sharing openly their perspectives on conflict. And they included, most importantly, a new focus on developing real relationships between students and teachers, knowing that trusting relationships are the very foundation of learning. A second administrative task is revising the curriculum so that it challenges the hidden messages of white supremacy rather than prolonging them. This involves being sure that the curriculum is not unduly focused on white achievement and white history but encompasses the stories of many cultures.

It should encompass the stories of resistance and liberation as well that are necessary to an understanding of the past and present. Our principals also took a hard look at how many African American students were being funneled into special education programs. There are other administrative factors as well. Principals should make sure that students are greeted every day by an array of faces, including ones that look like theirs. Instructional excellence and the ability to form warm connections are key, as Dr. Benjamin expressed, and white teachers can certainly learn how to relate to their diverse students.

But the evidence is clear that African American students do especially well when they are exposed to African American teachers and administrators; African American students who have these role models are significantly more likely to stay in school and to attend college. Even something as simple as the distribution of scholarship materials can require revision. Dr. Benjamin noticed that scholarship information was not being shared widely among his African American students. So he created an email system so that every student had an email address and every notice about scholarships and summer opportunities got sent to *all* students.

The third category of challenges for a turnaround principal is environmental factors. Children in poor communities face a host of poor health outcomes that are much more prevalent than among their counterparts in affluent schools and an increased risk of mental health challenges. Adverse childhood experiences contribute to many of these challenges. There may be toxic levels of stress that affect the students' ability to learn. Adverse childhood experiences may be heightened with exposure to violence, family members incarcerated, exposure to physical or verbal abuse, or experiences with racism that can lead to mental health crises for which the service accessibility is limited.

Also, there may be exposure to lead paint and contaminated water. A critically conscious principal must know the students, know the community, and be able to bring together district resources and community partners to bring vital services to the school. One of our principals, Mrs. Tonya, opened a school-based food pantry to address her students' food insecurities. The well-being of teachers is also critical. A principal has to be aware of teachers' stress and take every opportunity to support them in their best efforts. Teachers must convey optimism and belief in their students, and likewise principals must convey optimism and a belief in their teachers.

A laser focus on instructional quality is not incompatible with this. Good principals will support their teachers with professional development that is appropriate and differentiated for a turnaround setting, and not just a generic, boilerplate experience. They will also, like Dr. Jim, not hesitate to remove teachers who are communicating harmful stereotypes to students or resisting the changes needed to turn around the school.

Unfortunately, this is where the educational system differs greatly from the corporate world. During the process of trying to remove a teacher from a school or turnaround school, principals endure a great deal of stress from defiant teachers, unions, and district offices when attempting to remove a teacher. For students who desperately deserve an accomplished and effective teacher free from conventional thinking and with the skills at managing a classroom free from distractions, this is an unwanted barrier to learning.

***

This book offers an understanding to how critically conscious turnaround principals sustain the improvements of turnaround schools by unpacking equity in education, shedding light on the harm done when educators fail to recognize the need for an equitable education, and restoring and healing school communities. Principals can bring about great change, and they deserve the support of districts—not short-term demands and ever-mounting pressures without additional resources.

With better university preparation for a diverse classroom in the twenty-first century and a commitment by districts to hire critically conscious principals, turnaround schools can be successfully transformed. To make this a reality, educational scholars must apply themselves to researching leadership in turnaround schools. While many studies have examined the implementation and impact of programs and policies to improve the conditions and outcomes of turnaround schools, none has focused exclusively on the role of preparing school leaders to turn around chronically low-performing schools (Aladjem et al. 2018).

It is imperative to continue to expand the body of literature to gain an awareness of the plights and struggles of critically conscious turnaround principals. Future research might include a longitudinal study on how critically conscious principals improve and sustain the conditions of their turnaround schools. Dialogues and interviews with principals and district administrators may offer priceless insight into how they met the challenges of an equitable education. School improvement has been studied for decades, but there are significant gaps in the literature on school turnaround leadership.

And particularly the leadership demands of turnaround schools are a new and largely unexplored territory (Aladjem et al. 2018). Furthermore, an extensive exploration of principals' lived experiences of how they weather the challenges of turnaround schools will be key to understanding how many transformative educational leaders remain in their initial position and how many are removed by district leaders or simply relinquish their duties as principal.

A thorough understanding of the causes and effects of any turnaround principals' removal or resignation will help us understand how to sustain improvements rather than simply achieving short-term boosts. In support of this, we need quantitative comparative analyses of all regions of the country in order to determine the number of schools that have been successfully and sustainably transformed.

Quantitative comparative analysis is needed to analyze complex situations and determine why change happens in some cases but not others (Simister and Scholz 2017). A similar examination of current and future turnaround principals' competencies will help district leaders hire principals who are capable of identifying and eradicating the elements of systemic and structural racism that are embedded in the structures, policies, and procedures of their schools.

***

The need for social transformation is not a Black or white issue. It's a systemic issue in the educational system that warrants attention. All Americans will be impacted if the miseducation of students in turnaround schools is not confronted and addressed from solution-based perspectives. There is a great need for well-educated workers and thinkers, who have knowledge and skills. But the way to get there is through an educational system that has incorporated the lessons of social justice and equity, allowing all students to flourish and learn.

The education system has taken a blow during the pandemic. Virtual learning is a benefit for some students but a challenge and disadvantage to most. Furthermore, some students are not receiving the necessary supports for learning to continue because they have lost access to technology, social–emotional supports, and more. Teachers are overwhelmed too. There are anxieties and frustrations for principals and district administrators who are trying to balance the need for learning and the need for safety.

But the pandemic also provides a window of opportunity—a chance to alter "business as usual" and make lasting changes to our educational systems. All students have a civil right to an equitable education regardless of their zip code. Advocating for change in turnaround schools is "good trouble," as the late civil rights activist John Lewis liked to say. As a society, we must take the opportunity for change and run with it.

References

Akbar, Na'im. 1996. *Breaking the Chains of Psychological Slavery*. Tallahassee, FL: Mind Productions & Associates, Inc.

Aladjem, Dan, Adrienne von Glatz, Jeanine Hildreth, and Clarissa McKithen. 2018. "Leading Low-Performing Schools: Lessons from the Turnaround School Leaders Program." Report. Office of Planning, Evaluation, and Policy Development, Policy and Program Studies Service, US Department of Education, December. https://www2.ed.gov/rschstat/eval/teaching/leading-low-performing-schools/report.pdf.

Aladjem, Daniel K., Beatrice F. Birman, Martin Orland, Jenifer Harr-Robins, Alberto Heredia, Thomas B. Parrish, and Stephen J. Ruffini. 2010. "Achieving Dramatic School Improvement: An Exploratory Study; A Cross-Site Analysis from the Evaluation of Comprehensive School Reform Program Implementation and Outcomes Study." Cross-site analysis from the Evaluation of Comprehensive School Reform Program Implementation and Outcomes Study. US Department of Education, January. https://www2.ed.gov/rschstat/eval/other/dramatic-school-improvement/exploratory-study.pdf.

Alexander, Michelle. 2012. *The New Jim Crow: Mass Incarceration in the Age of Colorblindness*. New York: The New Press.

Alfonsi, Sharyn. 2020. "Early Results from 174 Flint Children Exposed to Lead during Water Crisis Shows 80% of Them Will Require Special Education Services." News. *60 Minutes*, March 15. https://www.cbsnews.com/news/flint-water-crisis-effect-on-children-60-minutes-2020–03–15/.

American Academy of Pediatrics. 2014. "Adverse Childhood Experiences and the Lifelong Consequences of Trauma." https://www.aap.org/en-us/documents/ttb_aces_consequences.pdf.

American Civil Liberties Union. 2014. "School-to-Prison Pipeline." Issues. Accessed March 1, 2021. https://www.aclu.org/issues/juvenile-justice/school-prison-pipeline/school-prison-pipeline?redirect=feature/school-prison-pipeline.

Andre-Bechely, Lois. 2005. "Public School Choice at the Intersection of Voluntary Integration and Not-So-Good Neighborhood Schools: Lessons from Parents' Experiences." *Educational Administration Quarterly* 41(2): 267–305.

Anyon, Jean 1997. *Ghetto Schooling: A Political Economy of Urban Educational Reform.* New York: Teachers College Press.

Asante, Molefi Kete. 2003. *Afrocentricity: The Theory of Social Change.* Revised and expanded. Chicago, IL: African American Images.

Atkins, Rebecca, and Alicia Oglesby. 2019. *Interrupting Racism: Equality and Social Justice in School Counseling.* New York: Routledge.

Aud, Susan, William Hussar, Michael Planty, Thomas Snyder, Kevin Bianco, Mary Ann Fox, Lauren Frohlich, Jana Kemp, and Lauren Drake. 2010. "The Condition of Education, 2010." Report. International Center for Education Statistics, Institute of Education Sciences, US Department of Education, NCES 2010-028, May. https://nces.ed.gov/pubs2010/2010028.pdf.

Backstrom, Brian. 2019. "School Turnaround Efforts: What's Been Tried, Why Those Efforts Failed, and What to Do Now." Report. Rockefeller Institute of Government, July. https://rockinst.org/wp-content/uploads/2019/07/7-23-19-School-Turnaround-Efforts.pdf.

Badger. 2017. "How Redlining's Racist Effects Lasted for Decades." The Upshot. *New York Times*, August 24. https://www.nytimes.com/2017/08/24/upshot/how-redlinings-racist-effects-lasted-for-decades.html.

Baptist, Edward. 2014. *The Half Has Never Been Told: Slavery and the Making of American Capitalism.* New York: Basic Books.

Battenfeld, Mary, and Felicity Crawford. 2015. "Why Every Student Succeeds Act Still Leaves Most Vulnerable Kids Behind." *The Conversation*, December 11. http://theconversation.com/what-every-student-succeeds-act-still-leaves-most-vulnerable-kids-behind-46247.

Berends, Mark, Susan Bodilly, and Sheila Nataraj Kirby. 2002. "Looking Back over a Decade of Whole-School Reform: The Experience of New American Schools." *Phi Delta Kappan* 84(2): 168–175. doi:10.1177/003172170208400214.

Biddle, Bruce J., and David C. Berliner. 2002. "A Research Synthesis/Unequal School Funding in the United States." *Beyond Instructional Leadership* 59(8): 48–59.

Bloom, Collette M., and David A. Erlandson. 2003. "African American Women Principals in Urban Schools: Realities, (Re)constructions, and Resolutions." *Educational Administration Quarterly* 39(3): 339–369.

Bloom, Howard S., Sandra Ham, Laura Melton, and Julieanne O'Brien. 2001. "Evaluating the Accelerated Schools Approach: A Look at Early Implementation and Impacts on Student Achievement in Eight Elementary Schools." With Fred C. Doolittle and Susan Kagehiro. Manpower Demonstration Research Corporation, November. https://www.mdrc.org/sites/default/files/full_94.pdf.

Bogotch, Ira. E. 2002. "Educational Leadership and Social Justice: Practice into Theory." *Journal of School Leadership* 12(2): 138–156.

Borman, Geoffrey D., Gina M. Hewes, Laura T. Overman, and Shelly Brown. 2003. "Comprehensive School Reform and Achievement: A Meta-Analysis." *Review of Educational Research* 73(2): 125–230. doi:10.3102/00346543073002125.

Boudreau, Emily. 2019. "School Discipline Linked to Later Consequences." *Usable Knowledge*, September 16. Harvard Graduate School of Education. https://www.gse.harvard.edu/news/uk/19/09/school-discipline-linked-later-consequences.

Boyatzis, Richard E. 1998. *Transforming Qualitative Information: Thematic Analysis and Code Development*. London: Sage.

Boyd, Brian. 2009. *On the Origin of Stories: Evolution, Cognition, and Fiction*. Cambridge, MA: The Belknap Press of Harvard University Press.

Boyes-Watson, Carolyn, and Kay Pranis. 2015. *Circle Forward: Building a Restorative School Community*. Saint Paul: Living Justice Press.

Brooks, Jeffrey S., and Mark T. Miles. 2006. "From Scientific Management to Social Justice . . . and Back Again? Pedagogical Shifts in the Study and Practice of Educational Leadership." *International Electronic Journal for Leadership in Learning* 10(21): 1–11.

Brooks, Jeffrey S., and George Theoharis, eds. 2019. *Whiteucation: Privilege, Power, and Prejudice in School and Society*. New York: Routledge.

Bryk, Anthony S., Penny Bender Sebring, Elaine Allensworth, Stuart Luppescu, and John Q. Easton, eds. 2010. *Organizing Schools for Improvement: Lessons from Chicago*. Chicago, IL and London: University of Chicago Press.

California Department of Education. 2020. "Behavior Intervention Strategies and Supports." Last reviewed November 19. https://www.cde.ca.gov/ls/ss/se/behaviorialintervention.asp.

Calkins, Andrew, William Guenther, Grace Belfiore, and Dave Lash. 2007. "The Turnaround Challenge: Why America's Best Opportunity to Dramatically Improve Student Achievement Lies in Our Worst-Performing Schools." Report. Mass Insight Education and Research Institute. https://www.massinsight.org/wp-content/uploads/2015/11/TheTurnaroundChallenge_MainReport.pdf.

Capper, Colleen A. 2019. *Organizational Theory for Equity and Diversity: Leading Integrated, Socially Just Education*. New York: Routledge.

Carlson, Dennis, and Michael W. Apple, eds. 1998. *Power/Knowledge/Pedagogy: The Meaning of Democratic Education in Unsettling Times*. Boulder, CO: Westview.

Center on Innovation and Improvement. 2010. "Information. Tools. Training." Lincoln, IL: Center on Innovation and Improvement, Academic Development Institute. http://www.centerii.org.

Centers for Disease Control and Prevention. 2021. "Preventing Adverse Childhood Experiences." *CDC.gov*, last reviewed April 6. https://www.cdc.gov/violenceprevention/aces/fastfact.html.

Chen, Grace. 2021. "An Overview of the Funding of Public Schools." *Public School Review*, updated March 31. https://www.publicschoolreview.com/blog/an-overview-of-the-funding-of-public-schools.

Clandinin, D. Jean. 2013. *Engaging in Narrative Inquiry*. New York: Routledge.

Corbin, Juliet M., and Anselm Strauss. 1990. "Grounded Theory Research: Procedures, Canons, and Evaluative Criteria." *Qualitative Sociology* 13(1): 3–21.

Creswell, John W., and Cheryl N. Poth. 2018. *Qualitative Inquiry and Research Design: Choosing among Five Approaches*, 4th edition. Thousand Oaks, CA: SAGE Publications, Inc.

Dantley, Michael. 2010. "Successful Leadership in Urban Schools: Principals and Critical Spirituality; A New Approach to Reform." *The Journal of Negro Education* 79(3): 214–219.

———. 2005. "The Power of Critical Spirituality to Act and to Reform." *Journal of School Leadership* 15(5): 500–518.

———. 2002. "Uprooting and Replacing Positivism, the Melting Pot, Multiculturalism, and Other Impotent Notions in Education Leadership through an African American Perspective." *Education and Urban Society* 34(3): 334–352.

Darling-Hammond, Linda. 2019. "America's School Funding Struggle: How We're Robbing Our Future by Under-investing in Our Children." *Forbes*, August 5. https://www.forbes.com/sites/lindadarlinghammond/2019/08/05/americas-school-funding-struggle-how-were-robbing-our-future-by-under-investing-in-our-children/#3fa3fed75eaf.

Darling-Hammond, Linda, Maria E. Hyler, and Madelyn Garnder. 2017. "Effective Teacher Professional Development." With assistance from Danny Espinoza. Research brief. Learning Policy Institute, June 5. https://learningpolicyinstitute.org/sites/default/files/product-files/Effective_Teacher_Professional_Development_REPORT.pdf.

David, Jane L. 2010. "Drastic School Turnaround Strategies Are Risky." *Interventions That Work* 68(2): 78–81.

Davis, Fania E. 2019. *The Little Book of Race and Restorative Justice: Black Lives, Healing, and US Social Transformation*. New York: Good Books.

de Brey, Cristobal, Lauren Musu, Joel McFarland, Sidney Wilkinson-Flicker, Melissa Diliberti, Anlan Zhang, Claire Branstetter, and Xiaolei Wang. 2019. "Status and Trends in the Education of Racial and Ethnic Groups, 2018." Report. National Center for Education Statistics, Institute of Education Sciences, US Department of Education, NCES 2019-038, February. https://nces.ed.gov/pubs2019/2019038.pdf.

Degruy, Joy. (2005) 2017. *Post Traumatic Slave Syndrome: America's Legacy of Enduring Injury and Healing*, revised edition. [N.p.]: Joy DeGruy Publications, Inc.

Delpit, Lisa. 1995. *Other People's Children: Cultural Conflict in the Classroom*. New York: The New Press.

DeMatthews, David E. 2015. "Making Sense of Social Justice Leadership: A Case Study of a Principal's Experiences to Create a More Inclusive School." *Leadership and Policy in Schools* 14(2): 139–166. doi:10.1080/15700763.2014.997939.

Dillard, Cynthia B. 1995. "Leading with Her Life: An African American Feminist (Re)Interpretation of Leadership for an Urban High School Principal." *Educational Leadership Quarterly* 31(4): 539–563. doi:10.1177%2F0013161X9503100403.

Dimitriadis, Greg, and Dennis Carlson. 2003. *Promises to Keep: Cultural Studies, Democratic Education, and Public Life*. New York: Routledge Falmer.

Dunn, Lenay, and Eric Ambroso. 2019. "Balancing Act: State and District Roles in School Improvement under ESSA." Center on School Turnaround, WestEd, September 19. https://csti.wested.org/wp-content/uploads/2019/09/CST-Balancing-Act-Brief_FINAL.pdf.

Edutopia. 2019. "The Power of Relationships in School." Video and transcript. How Learning Happens series. January 14. https://www.edutopia.org/video/power-rel ationships-schools.

El-Amin, Aaliyah, Scott Seider, Daren Graves, Jalene Tamerat, Shelby Clark, Madora Soutter, Jamie Johannsen, and Saira Malhotra. 2017. "Critical Consciousness: A Key to Student Achievement." *Phi Delta Kappan* 98(5): 18–23. https://kappano nline.org/critical-consciousness-key-student-achievement/.

English, Fenwick. 2008. *Anatomy of Professional Practice: Promising Research Perspectives on Educational Leadership*. Lanham, MD: Rowman & Littlefield Education.

English, Fenwick, and Rosemary Papa. 2010. *Restoring Human Agency to Educational Administration: Status and Strategies*. Thousand Oaks, CA: Sage Publications.

Fairchild, Tierney Temple, and Jo Lynne DeMary. 2011. *The Turnaround Mindset: Aligning Leadership for Student Success*. Lanham, MD: Rowman & Littlefield Education.

Fenning, Pamela, and Jennifer Rose. 2007. "Overrepresentation of African American Students in Exclusionary Discipline: The Role of School Policy." *Urban Education* 42(6): 536–559. doi:10.1177%2F0042085907305039.

Fine, Michelle. 1994. "Distance and Other Stances: Negotiations of Power Inside Feminist Research." In *Power and Method: Political Activism and Educational Research*, edited by Andrew Gitlin, 13–35. London: Routledge.

Frankenberg, Erica and Genevieve Seigel-Hawley. 2008. "Are Teachers Prepared for Racially Changing Schools: Teachers Describe Their Preparation, Resources, and Practices for Racially Diverse Schools." The Civil Rights Project and Southern Poverty Law Center. January. https://www.civilrightsproject.ucla.edu/research/k -12-education/integration-and-diversity/are-teachers-prepared-for-racially-chang ing-schools/frankenberg-are-teachers-prepared-racially.pdf.

Freire, Paulo. (1970) 2000. *Pedagogy of the Oppressed*. New York: Bloomsbury Publishing, Inc.

Furman, Gail. 2012. "Social Justice Leadership as Praxis: Developing Capacities through Preparation Programs." *Educational Administration Quarterly* 48(2): 191–229. doi:10.1177%2F0013161X11427394.

Gale de Saxe, Jennifer. 2019. "Complicating Resistance: Intersectionality, Liberation, and Democracy." In *Educating for Critical Consciousness*, edited by George Yancy, 127–145. New York: Routledge.

Gershenson, Seth, Stephen B. Holt, and Nicholas Papageorge. 2015. "Who Believes in Me? The Effect of Student-Teacher Demographic Match on Teacher Expectations." Working paper. Upjohn Institute, no. 15-231, July 1. https://research.upjohn.org/cg i/viewcontent.cgi?article=1248&context=up_workingpapers.

Gill, Brian P., Ron W. Zimmer, Jolley Christman, and Suzanne Blanc. 2007. "State Takeover, School Restructuring, Private Management, and Student Achievement in Philadelphia." Monograph series. RAND Education and Research for Action, RAND Corporation. https://www.rand.org/content/dam/rand/pubs/monographs/2 007/RAND_MG533.pdf.

Gillborn, David. 2008. *Racism and Education: Coincidence or Conspiracy?* New York: Routledge.

Gooden, Mark A., and Michael Dantley. 2012. "Centering Race in a Framework for Leadership Preparation." *Journal of Research on Leadership Education* 7(2): 237–253.

Gordon, Nora. 2017. "Race, Poverty, and Interpreting Overrepresentation in Special Education." Report. *Brookings*, September 20. https://www.brookings.edu/research/race-poverty-and-interpreting-overrepresentation-in-special-education.

Grissom, Jason A., Anna J. Egalite, and Constance A. Lindsay. 2021. "How Principals Affect Students and Schools: A Systematic Synthesis of Two Decades of Research." Research report. The Wallace Foundation, February. https://www.wallacefoundation.org/knowledge-center/Documents/How-Principals-Affect-Students-and-Schools.pdf.

Gross, Betheny, T. Kevin Booker, and Dan Goldhaber. 2009. "Boosting Student Achievement: The Effect of Comprehensive School Reform on Student Achievement." *Educational Evaluation and Policy Analysis* 31(2): 111–126. https://journals.sagepub.com/doi/10.3102/0162373709333886.

Guo, Jeff. 2016. "American Has Locked Up So Many Black People It Has Warped Our Sense of Reality." *Washington Post*, February 26. https://www.washingtonpost.com/news/wonk/wp/2016/02/26/america-has-locked-up-so-many-black-people-it-has-warped-our-sense-of-reality/.

Hambrick Hitt, Dallas, Dennis Woodruff, Coby V. Meyers, and Guorong Zhu. 2018. "Principal Competencies that Make a Difference: Identifying a Model for Leaders of School Turnaround." *Journal of School Leadership* 28(1): 56–81.

Harbatkin, E., and G. T. Henry. 2019. "The Cascading Effects of Principal Turnover on Students and Schools." Brown Center Chalkboard. *Brookings* (blog), October 21. https://www.brookings.edu/blog/brown-center-chalkboard/2019/10/21/the-cascading-effects-of-principal-turnover-on-students-and-schools/.

Harris, Rebecca. 2014. "For the Record: Turnaround Principal Turnover." Contributions by Jenna Frasier. *The Chicago Reporter*, January 14. https://www.chicagoreporter.com/record-turnaround-principal-turnover/.

Harvard Graduate School of Education. N.d. "School Turnaround Leaders." *Harvard.edu*, accessed April 21, 2021. https://www.gse.harvard.edu/ppe/program/school-turnaround-leaders.

Herman, Rebecca, Priscilla Dawson, Thomas Dee, Jay Greene, Rebecca Maynard, Sam Redding, and Marlene Darwin. 2008. "Turning Around Chronically Low-Performing Schools: A Practice Guide." Report. National Center for Education Evaluation and Regional Assistance, Institute of Education Sciences, US Department of Education, NCEE 2008-4020, May. https://ies.ed.gov/ncee/wwc/Docs/PracticeGuide/Turnaround_pg_04181.pdf.

Hilliard, Asa, III. 1991. "Do We Have the Will to Educate All Children?" *Educational Leadership* 49(1): 31–36.

Horsford, Sonya Douglass. 2011. *Learning in a Burning House: Educational Inequality, Ideology, and (Dis)Integration*. New York: Teachers College Press.

Howell, William G. 2015. "Results of President Obama's Race to the Top: Win or Lose, States Enacted Education Reforms." *Education Next* 15(4): 1–12. https://www.educationnext.org/results-president-obama-race-to-the-top-reform/.

Hurlburt, Steven, Susan Bowles Therriault, and Kerstin Carlson Le Floch. 2012. "School Improvement Grants: Analyses of State Applications and Eligible and Awarded Schools." Report. National Center for Education Evaluation and Regional Assistance, Institute of Education Sciences, US Department of Education, NCEE 2012-4060, October. https://ies.ed.gov/ncee/pubs/20124060/pdf/20124060.pdf.

Jacob, Brian A. 2017. "How the U.S. Department of Education Can Foster Education Reform in the Era of Trump and ESSA." Report. *Brookings*, February 2. https://www.brookings.edu/research/how-the-u-s-department-of-education-can-foster-education-reform-in-the-era-of-trump-and-essa/.

Jamieson, Kerry. 2020. "Aces and Children's Environment." Blog. Center for Child Counseling, July 24. https://www.centerforchildcounseling.org/aces-and-childrens-environments/.

Jan, Tracy. 2018. "Redlining Was Banned 50 Years Ago. It's Still Hurting Minorities Today." *Washington Post*, March 28. https://www.washingtonpost.com/news/wonk/wp/2018/03/28/redlining-was-banned-50-years-ago-its-still-hurting-minorities-today/.

Kamenetz, Anya. 2018. "DeVos to Rescind Obama-Era Guidance on School Discipline." *All Things Considered*, December 18. https://www.npr.org/2018/12/18/675556455/devos-to-rescind-obama-era-guidance-on-school-discipline.

Kendi, Ibram. 2019. *How to Be an Antiracist*. New York: One World.

Kim, Jeong-Hee. 2015. *Understanding Narrative Inquiry: The Crafting and Analysis of Stories as Research*. Thousand Oaks, CA: SAGE Publications, Inc.

Kim, Catherine Y., Daniel J. Losen, and Damon T. Hewitt. 2010. *The School-to-Prison Pipeline: Structuring Legal Reform*. New York: New York University Press.

Kincheloe, Joe L., and Shirley R. Steinberg. 1997. *Changing Multiculturalism: New Times, New Curriculum*. Buckingham: Open University Press.

King, Joyce E. 1991. "Dysconscious Racism: Ideology, Identity, and the Miseducation of Teachers." *The Journal of Negro Education* 60(2):133–146. doi:10.2307/2295605.

Klein, Alyson. 2019. "States Hunt for Evidence to Underpin School Turnaround Efforts." *Education Week* 38(27): 16–19. https://www.edweek.org/ew/articles/2019/04/03/states-hunt-for-evidence-to-underpin-school.html.

Koenig, Rebecca. 2020. "How to Be an Antiracist Educator: An Interview with Ibram X. Kendi." *EdSurge*, December 1. https://www.edsurge.com/news/2020-12-01-how-to-be-an-antiracist-educator-an-interview-with-ibram-x-kendi.

Kowal, Julia M., and Emily Ayscue Hassel. 2005. "Turnarounds with New Leaders and Staff: School Restructuring Options Under No Child Left Behind." What Works When? series. The Center for Comprehensive School Reform and Improvement. https://files.eric.ed.gov/fulltext/ED502903.pdf.

Kowal, Julie, Emily Ayscue Hassel, and Bryan C. Hassel. 2009. "Successful School Turnarounds: Seven Steps for District Leaders." *Issue Brief*, September 15. The

Center for Comprehensive School Reform and Improvement. https://files.eric.ed.gov/fulltext/ED507589.pdf.
Kunjufu, Jawanza. 2006. *An African Centered Response to Ruby Payne's Poverty Theory*. Chicago, IL: African American Images.
Kutash, Jeff, Eva Nico, Emily Gorin, Samira Rahmatullah, and Kate Tallant. 2010. "The School Turnaround Field Guide." FSG Social Impact Advisors, September. https://www.wallacefoundation.org/knowledge-center/Documents/The-School-Turnaround-Field-Guide.pdf.
Ladson-Billings, Gloria. 2020. "Just What Is Critical Race Theory, and What's It Doing in a Nice Field like Education?" In *The Gloria Ladson-Billings Reader*, edited by Abul Pitre, Tanya Hudson, Jocelyn Smith-Gray, and Kishia Carrington James, 44–67. San Diego: Cognella.
———. 2007. "Pushing Past the Achievement Gap: An Essay on the Language Deficit." *The Journal of Negro Education* 76(3): 316–323. https://www.jstor.org/stable/40034574?seq=1.
———. 2006. "From the Achievement Gap to the Education Debt: Understanding Achievement in U.S. Schools." Presidential address. *Educational Researcher* 35(7): 3–12. https://www.jstor.org/stable/3876731.
———. 2000. "Fighting for Our Lives: Preparing Teachers to Teach African American Students." *Journal of Teacher Education* 51(3): 206–214.
Ladson-Billings, Gloria, and William F. Tate. 2020. "Toward a Critical Race Theory in Education." In *The Gloria Ladson-Billings Reader*, edited by Abul Pitre, Tanya Hudson, Jocelyn Smith-Gray, and Kishia Carrington James, 22–43. San Diego: Cognella.
Leachman, Michael, Nick Albares, Kathleen Masterson, and Marlana Wallace. 2016. "Most States Have Cut School Funding, and Some Continue Cutting." Report. Center on Budget and Policy Priorities, revised January 25. https://www.cbpp.org/research/state-budget-and-tax/most-states-have-cut-school-funding-and-some-continue-cutting.
Leithwood, Kenneth, Alma Harris, and Tiiu Strauss. 2010. *Leading School Turnaround: How Successful Leaders Transform Low-Performing Schools*. San Francisco: Jossey-Bass.
Levin, Stephanie, Kathryn Bradley, and Caitlin Scott. 2019. "Principal Turnover: Insights from Current Principals." Research brief. Learning Policy Institute, National Association of Secondary School Principals. https://learningpolicyinstitute.org/sites/default/files/product-files/NASSP_LPI_Insights_Principals_BRIEF.pdf.
Libassi, C. J. 2018. "The Neglected College Race Gap: Racial Disparities among College Completers." Center for American Progress, May 23. https://cdn.americanprogress.org/content/uploads/2018/05/22135501/CollegeCompletions-Brief1.pdf?_ga=2.179634468.1684561591.1619305451-539321054.1619305451.
Losen, Daniel J., and Paul Martinez. 2021. "Lost Opportunities: How Disparate School Discipline Continues to Drive Differences in the Opportunity to Learn." Report. Learning Policy Institute, Center for Civil Rights Remedies at the Civil Rights Project, UCLA, last revised February 17. https://www.civilrightsproject

.ucla.edu/research/k-12-education/school-discipline/lost-opportunities-how-dispa
rate-school-discipline-continues-to-drive-differences-in-the-opportunity-to-learn/
Lost-Opportunities-REPORT-v17.pdf.

Lunder, Sonya. 2017. "Drinking Water and Children's Health." Research. Environmental Working Group, July 26. https://www.ewg.org/research/drinking-water-and-childrens-health.

Luster, Sara. 2018. "How Exclusionary Discipline Creates Disconnected Students." *NEA Today*, July 19. https://www.nea.org/advocating-for-change/new-from-nea/how-exclusionary-discipline-creates-disconnected-students.

Martin, Wallace. 1986. *Recent Theories of Narrative*. Ithaca, NY: Cornell University Press.

McFarland, Joel, Bill Hussar, Jijun Zhang, Xiaolei Wang, Ke Wang, Sarah Hein, Melissa Diliberti, Emily Forrest Cataldi, Farrah Bullock Mann, and Amy Barmer. 2019. "The Condition of Education, 2019." Report. International Center for Education Statistics, Institute of Education Sciences, US Department of Education, NCES 2019-144, May. https://nces.ed.gov/pubs2019/2019144.pdf.

McIntyre, Erin. 2016. "Decaying School Buildings Have Physical, Psychological Consequences." Deep Dive. *K–12 Dive*, April 13. https://www.k12dive.com/news/decaying-school-buildings-have-physical-psychological-consequences/417119/.

Meyers, Coby V., and Dallas Hambrick Hitt. 2017. "School Turnaround Principals: What Does Initial Research Literature Suggest They Are Doing to Be Successful?" *Journal of Education for Students Placed at Risk* 22(1): 38–56. doi:10.1080/10824669.2016.1242070.

Milner, H. Richard, IV. 2015. *Rac(e)ing to Class: Confronting Poverty and Race in Schools and Classrooms*. Cambridge, MA: Harvard Education Press.

———. 2010. *Start Where You Are, but Don't Stay There: Understanding Diversity, Opportunity Gaps, and Teaching in Today's Classrooms*. Cambridge, MA: Harvard Education Press.

Minnesota Department of Education. N.d. "Restorative Practices." Accessed March 3, 2021. https://education.mn.gov/MDE/dse/safe/prac/.

Mitchell, Bruce, and Juan Franco. 2018. "HOLC 'Redlining' Maps: The Persistent Structure of Segregation and Economic Inequality." National Community Reinvestment Coalition, February. https://ncrc.org/wp-content/uploads/dlm_uploads/2018/02/NCRC-Research-HOLC-10.pdf.

Morrison, Nick. 2019. "Black Students 'Face Racial Bias' in School Discipline." *Forbes*, August 5. https://www.forbes.com/sites/nickmorrison/2019/04/05/black-students-face-racial-bias-in-school-discipline/?sh=58b478ee36d5.

National Dropout Prevention Center. N.d. "Early Childhood Education." Accessed January 5, 2021. https://dropoutprevention.org/effective-strategies/early-childhood-education/.

Oakland Unified School District. 2020. "The Pandemic of Racism: How Does White Supremacy Show Up in Our Schools." PowerPoint presentation. *OUSD.org*, August 6. https://www.ousd.org/cms/lib/CA01001176/Centricity/Domain/4433/8.6.20%20The%20Pandemic%20of%20Racism%20-%20how%20white%20supremacy%20shows%20up%20in%20our%20schools.pdf.

Obama, Barack. 2010. Remarks by the President in State of the Union Address. *ObamaWhiteHouse.archives.gov*, January 27. https://obamawhitehouse.archives.gov/the-press-office/remarks-president-state-union-address.

O'Dowd, Mary Frances. 2020. "Explainer: What Is Systemic Racism and Institutional Racism?" *The Conversation*, February 4. https://theconversation.com/explainer-what-is-systemic-racism-and-institutional-racism-131152.

Osborne, David. 2016. "Holding Schools Accountable: School Performance Standards Are Outdated. Here Are Six Ways We Can Improve Them." Opinion. *U.S. News and World Report*, October 7, pp. 1–15. https://www.usnews.com/opinion/articles/2016-10-07/6-ways-to-hold-schools-accountable-under-the-every-student-succeeds-act.

Papa, Rosemary, and Fenwick W. English. 2011. *Turnaround Principals for Underperforming Schools*. Plymouth, UK: Rowman & Littlefield Education.

Parrett, William H., and Kathleen M. Budge, eds. 2012. *Turning High-Poverty Schools into High-Performing Schools*. Alexandria, VA: Association for Supervision and Curriculum Development.

Petrella, Christopher. 2017. "The Resegregation of America: The Consequences of Creeping Racial Resegregation Constitute Nothing Less than a National Crisis." Think. *NBC News*, December 3. https://www.nbcnews.com/think/opinion/resegregation-america-ncna801446.

Pham, Lam, Gary T. Henry, Ron Zimmer, and Adam Kho. 2018. "School Turnaround after Five Years: An Extended Evaluation of Tennessee's Achievement School District and Local Innovation Zones." TN Education Research Alliance, June. https://peabody.vanderbilt.edu/TERA/files/School_Turnaround_After_Five_Years_FINAL.pdf.

Pinderhughes, Howard, Rachel A. Davis, and Myesha Williams. 2015. "Adverse Community Experiences and Resilience: A Framework for Addressing and Preventing Community Trauma." Prevention Institute, February. https://www.preventioninstitute.org/publications/adverse-community-experiences-and-resilience-framework-addressing-and-preventing.

Pitre, Abul. 2018. *Farrakhan and Education*. San Diego: Cognella, Inc.

———. 2015. *The Education Philosophy of Elijah Muhammad: Education for a New World*, 3rd edition. Lanham, MD: Hamilton Books.

———. 2014. *Education Leaders in a Multicultural Society: A Critical Perspective*. San Diego: Cognella, Inc.

———. 2011. *Freedom Fighters: Struggles Instituting the Study of Black History in K–12 Education*. San Diego: Cognella, Inc.

Pitre, Abul, and Jocelyn Smith-Gray. 2020. "Preparing Educational Leaders for Social Justice: The Case of Historically Black Colleges and Universities." In *Handbook on Promoting Social Justice in Education*, edited by Rosemary Papa, 1899–1900. New York: Springer. https://link.springer.com/content/pdf/10.1007/978-3-030-14625-2_85.pdf.

Pitre, Abul, Tawannah G. Allen, and Esrom Pitre, eds. 2015. *Multicultural Education for Educational Leaders*. Lanham, MD: Rowman & Littlefield.

ProCon.org. 2020. "History of Standardized Tests." Pro.Con/Encyclopedia Britannica, Inc., updated December 7. https://standardizedtests.procon.org/history-of-standardized-tests/.

Quaglia Institute for School Voice and Aspirations. 2016. "School Voice Report, 2016." https://quagliainstitute.org/dmsView/School_Voice_Report_2016.

Quereshi, Ajmel, and Jason Okonofua. 2017. "Locked Out of the Classroom: How Implicit Bias Contributes to Disparities in School Discipline." Report. The NAACP Legal Defense and Education Fund, Inc., November 30. https://www.naacpldf.org/files/about-us/Bias_Reportv2017_30_11_FINAL.pdf.

Rapp, Dana. 2002. "Social Justice and the Importance of Rebellious, Oppositional Imaginations." *Journal of School Leadership* 12(3): 226–245.

Rhim, Lauren Morando, and Sam Redding, eds. 2014. "The State Role in School Turnaround: Emerging Best Practices." The Center on School Turnaround, WestEd, February 11. https://csti.wested.org/wp-content/uploads/2018/04/The_State_Role_in_School_Turnaround.pdf.

Riessman, Catherine Kohler. 2008. *Narrative Methods for the Human Sciences.* Thousand Oaks, CA: SAGE Publications.

Rose, Matthew. 2017. "The Idea of the 'Banking Concept in Education." *OurPolitics.net*, April 19. https://ourpolitics.net/the-idea-of-the-banking-concept-in-education/.

SAMHSA (Substance Abuse and Mental Health Services). 2015. "The National Child Traumatic Stress Initiative: Helping Kids Recover and Thrive." SAMHSA and National Child Traumatic Stress Initiative, https://www.samhsa.gov/sites/default/files/programs_campaigns/nctsi/nctsi-trifold-brochure-single.pdf.

Schwalbach, Jude. 2018. "Federal Education Programs Are Bloated and Failing: Now, Congress Wants to Give Them More Money." Commentary. The Heritage Foundation, September 25. https://www.heritage.org/education/commentary/federal-education-programs-are-bloated-and-failing-now-congress-wants-give.

Seider, Scott, and Daren Graves. 2020. *Schooling for Critical Consciousness: Engaging Black and Latinx Youth in Analyzing, Navigating, and Challenging Racial Injustice.* Cambridge, MA: Harvard Education Press.

Shields, Carolyn M. 2003. *Good Intentions Are Not Enough: Transformative Leadership for Communities of Difference.* Lanham, MD: Scarecrow Press.

Shuster, Kate. 2018. *Teaching Hard History: American Slavery.* Montgomery, AL: The Southern Poverty Law Center.

Simister, Nigel, and Vera Scholz. 2017. "Qualitative Comparative Analysis (QCA)." Paper. INTRAC, January. https://www.intrac.org/wpcms/wp-content/uploads/2017/01/Qualitative-comparative-analysis.pdf.

Slack, Megan, and Alicia Oken. 2014. "A Child's Course in Life Should Be Determined Not by the Zip Code She's Born In." *ObamaWhiteHouse.archives.gov*, blog, January 10. https://obamawhitehouse.archives.gov/blog/2014/01/10/president-obama-child-s-course-life-should-be-determined-not-zip-code-she-s-born.

Sleeter, Christine E. 2012. "Confronting the Marginalization of Culturally Responsive Pedagogy." *Urban Education* 47(3): 562–584. doi:10.1177%2F0042085911431472.

Smarick, Andy. 2010. "The Turnaround Fallacy." *Education Next* 10(1): 20–26. https://www.educationnext.org/the-turnaround-fallacy/.

Sparks, Sarah D., "Why Teacher-Student Relationships Matter," *EducationWeek*, March 19, 2009, https://www.edweek.org/teaching-learning/why-teacher-student-relationships-matter/2019/03.

Spring, Joel. 2011. *The Politics of American Education*. New York: Routledge.

Steiner, Lucy M., Emily Ayscue Hassel, Bryan C. Hassel, Shonaka Ellison, Kathleen St. Louis, Alan Anderson, Brian Sims, and Melissa DeBartolo. (2008) 2016. "School Turnaround Leaders: Competencies for Success." School Turnaround Collection. Public Impact, updated September. https://publicimpact.com/wp-content/uploads/2009/09/Turnaround_Leader_Competencies.pdf.

Steiner, Lucy, and Sharon Kebschull Barrett. 2012. "Turnaround Principal Competencies." *School Administrator* 69(7): 26–29. https://eric.ed.gov/?id=EJ982370.

Stephens, Verlan. 2018. "Federal Education Funding, Explained." *Selling to Schools*, Agile Education Marketing, June 27. https://sellingtoschools.com/education-management/federal-education-funding-explained/.

Stotsky, Sandra. 2018. "Why Educational Policies Fail: The Elephant in the Family Room." *New Boston Post*, May 3, pp. 1–6. https://newbostonpost.com/2018/05/03/why-educational-policies-fail-the-elephant-in-the-family-room/.

Straus, Chelsea, and Tiffany D. Miller. 2016. "Strategies to Improve Low-Performing Schools under the Every Student Succeeds Act: How 3 Districts Found Success Using Evidence-Based Practices." Report. Center for American Progress, March. https://cdn.americanprogress.org/wp-content/uploads/2016/03/01075517/NonCharterSchools-report.pdf.

Strunk, Katharine O., Julie A. Marsh, Ayesha K. Hashim, Susan Bush-Mecenas, and Tracey Weinstein. 2016. "The Impact of Turnaround Reform on Student Outcomes: Evidence and Insights from the Los Angeles Unified School District." *Education Finance and Policy* 11(3): 251–282. http://www.mitpressjournals.org/doi/abs/10.1162/EDFP_a_00188.

Stuit, David A. 2010. "Are Bad Schools Immortal? The Scarcity of Turnarounds and Shutdowns in Both Charter and District Sectors." Foreword by Chester E. Finn Jr. and Amber M. Winkler. Study. Thomas B. Fordham Institute, December 14. Available for download at https://fordhaminstitute.org/national/research/are-bad-schools-immortal.

Suitts, Steve. 2013. "A New Majority Update: Low-Income Students in the South and Nation." Research report update. Southern Education Foundation, October. https://www.southerneducation.org/wp-content/uploads/2019/02/New-Majority-2013.pdf.

Taylor. Edward. 2009. "The Foundations of Critical Race Theory in Education. An Introduction." In *Foundation of Critical Race Theory in Education*, edited by Edward Taylor, David Gillborn, and Gloria Ladson-Billings, 1–16. New York: Routledge.

Theoharis, George. 2019. "White Privilege and Educational Leadership." In *Whiteucation: Privilege, Power, and Prejudice in School and Society*, edited by Jeffrey S. Brooks and George Theoharis, 52–61. New York: Routledge.

———. 2010. "Disrupting Injustice: Principals Narrate the Strategies They Use to Improve Their Schools and Advance Social Justice." *Teachers College Record* 112(1): 331–373.

———. 2009. *The School Leaders Our Children Deserve: Seven Keys to Equity, Social Justice, and School Reform.* New York: Teachers College Press.

———. 2007. "Social Justice Educational Leaders and Resistance: Toward a Theory of Social Justice Leadership. *Educational Administrative Quarterly* 43(2): 221–258.

Theoharis, George, and Marcelle Haddix. 2011. "Undermining Racism and a Whiteness Ideology: White Principals Living a Commitment to Equitable and Excellent Schools." *Urban Education* 46(6): 1332–1351. doi:10.1177/0042085911416012.

Think:Kids. N.d. "Collaborative Problem Solving® (CPS)." Accessed March 3, 2021. https://thinkkids.org/cps-overview.

Thomas, David R. 2006. "A General Inductive Approach for Analyzing Qualitative Evaluation Data." *American Journal of Evaluation* 27(2): 237–246.

Turner, Cory. 2015. "No Child Left Behind: What Worked, What Didn't." NPR Ed. *Morning Edition*, October 27. https://www.npr.org/sections/ed/2015/10/27/443110755/no-child-left-behind-what-worked-what-didn't.

Tyre, Peg. 2015. "Why Do More than Half of Principals Quit after Five Years? New Principal Struggles to Find balance in Ever-Changing Role." *The Hechinger Report*, September 26. https://hechingerreport.org/why-do-more-than-half-of-principals-quit-after-five-years/.

Underhill, Megan R., David L. Brunsma, and W. Carson Byrd. 2019. "White Privilege and American Society: The State, White Opportunity Hoarding, and Inequality." In *Whiteucation: Privilege, Power, and Prejudice in School and Society*, edited by Jeffrey S. Brooks and George Theoharis, 52–61. New York: Routledge.

United States Department of Education. 2017. "Investing in Innovation Fund (i3)." About ED: Offices. *ED.gov*, last modified June 21. https://www2.ed.gov/programs/innovation/index.html.

———. 2016. "School Improvement Grants: Resources Information." Programs. *ED.gov*, last modified June 1. https://www2.ed.gov/programs/sif/resources.html.

———. 2015. "Fact Sheet: Congress Acts to Fix No Child Left Behind." Archived Information. *ED.gov*, December 15. https://www.ed.gov/news/press-releases/fact-sheet-congress-acts-fix-no-child-left-behind.

———. 2014. "U.S. Departments of Education and Justice Release School Discipline Guidance Package to Enhance School Climate and Improve School Discipline Policies/Practices." Archived Information. ED.gov, January 8. https://www.ed.gov/news/press-releases/us-departments-education-and-justice-release-school-discipline-guidance-package-.

———. 2011. *An Overview of School Turnaround*. Washington, D.C.: Office of Education, 2011. https://www2.ed.gov/programs/sif/sigoverviewppt.pdf.

———. 2009. "Race to the Top." Programs. *ED.gov*, last modified December 29. https://www2.ed.gov/programs/racetothetop/factsheet.html.

US Government Accountability Office. 2019. "K-12 Education: Certain Groups of Students Attend Alternative Schools in Greater Proportions than They Do Other

Schools." Report to the chair, GAO-19-373, July 15. https://www.gao.gov/assets/gao-19-373.pdf.

Valles, Brenda, and Daniel M. Miller. 2010. "How Leadership and Discipline Policies Color School-Community Relationships: A Critical Race Theory Analysis." *Journal of School Public Relations* 31(4): 319–341.

Wallace Foundation, staff. 2011. "Research Findings to Support Effective Educational Policies: A Guide for Policy Makers," 2nd edition. The Wallace Foundation, March. https://www.wallacefoundation.org/knowledge-center/Documents/Findings-to-Support-Effective-Educational-Policy-Making.pdf.

Wang, Karla. 2019. "Teacher Turnover: Why It's Problematic and How Administrators Can Address It." *The Science of Learning Blog*, July 19. https://www.scilearn.com/teacher-turnover/.

Wilson, Camille, and Lauri Johnson. 2015. "Black Educational Activism for Community Empowerment: International Leadership Perspectives." *International Journal of Multicultural Education* 17(1): 102–120. https://ijme-journal.org/index.php/ijme/article/viewFile/963/1035.

Woodson, C. (1933) 2018. *The Mis-education of the Negro*. Middletown, DE: Book Tree.

Yu, Eric, and Pamela Cantor. 2016. "Turnaround for Children: Poverty, Stress, Schools; Implications for Research, Practice, and Assessment." Turnaround USA, May. http://www.turnaroundusa.org/wp-content/uploads/2016/05/Turnaround-for-Children-Poverty-Stress-Schools.pdf.

Index

ACE Quiz, 16
ACEs. *See* adverse childhood experiences (ACEs)
achievement gaps, 5, 28
Achievement School District (ASD), 11, 12
Adequate Yearly Progress (AYP), 4
administrative practices, 29, 30
administrative skills, 55
adverse childhood experiences (ACEs), xx, 16, 31, 32, 80
African American(s), xx, xxii, 2, 29, 39, 63; cultural history of, 39; males, 29–31, 44, 74; schools, 40, 56, 57; students, xix–xxi, 2, 24–25, 28–32, 35, 39, 43, 44, 46, 47, 63, 66, 67, 69, 70, 72, 74, 76–78, 80; teachers, 63, 65, 79, 80
African-centered curriculum, 39
air quality, 3
American Academy of Pediatrics, 33
American capitalism, 39
American Dream, 31
American Recovery and Reassessment Act (ARRA, 2009), 4–6, 8, 9, 21, 53
American slavery, 31, 32, 39
America's Promise Alliance, 47
Annual National Conference of State Legislators (2019), 2

antiracist educational curriculum, 40
ARRA. *See* American Recovery and Reassessment Act (ARRA, 2009)
Asante, Molefi Kete, 39
ASD. *See* Achievement School District (ASD)
Atkins, Rebecca, 61
AYP. *See* Adequate Yearly Progress (AYP)

Backstrom, Brian, 14
Band-Aid approach, 15
"banking concept," 65, 69
Barbic, Chris, 11, 12
behavior referrals, 70, 71
Black Codes, 31
Black education, 28, 31
Black history, 25
Black History Month, 25, 39
brain development, 15, 33, 49, 67
"breaking the silence" approach, 56, 57
Brookings Institution, 53
Bush, George W., 4
Bush administration, 4

California Department of Education, 48
"Case Studies of Schools Receiving School Improvement Grants Final Report," 9

97

The Center for Promise, 47
Center on Budget and Policy Priorities, 12
Center on Innovation and Improvement, 7
Centers for Disease Control and Prevention, 31
Chicago Public Schools, 53
civil rights groups, 8
classroom dynamics, 18
classroom instructional time, 43–44, 79
classroom management, 16
collaborative problem solving (CPS) approach, 41–43, 71
Common Core standards, 7
Condition of Education (2019), 2
conflict circle. *See* restorative justice circle
contaminated water systems, 34, 80
COVID-19 pandemic, xix, 48, 82
CPS. *See* collaborative problem solving (CPS) approach
criminal justice system, 30, 46
critical consciousness, xxi, xxii, 24–26, 29, 34, 35, 38, 39, 52, 54–56, 63, 65, 75, 77, 78
critically conscious principal, xxi–xxiii, 26–34, 37, 43, 44, 55–56, 64, 76, 81; administrative factors, 29–31, 78, 80; attending to mental health, 44–46; attitudinal factors, 26–29; culturally relevant curricula and multicultural education practices, 38–40; environmental factors, 31–34, 80; experiential preparation programs and, 73–75; importance of, 57–75; leadership work, 52–54; prioritizing instructional time, 43–44, 79; professional development of staff, 49–52; punitive discipline and restorative justice discipline, 46–49, 79; relationship-building, 42–43; scope of, 37–38; student agency and voices, 40–42
critical thinking skills, 25

culturally relevant curricula, 38–40, 54, 69
culture: identities, 32; incongruence, 67, 72
curriculum reform, 39, 80
Curry School of Education, 7

Dantley, Michael, 35, 50
Darden School of Business, 7
Darling-Hammond, Linda, 42
deficit thinking, 64–66, 78
Degruy, Joy, 63
Denver Public School District (DPS), 19
Department of Justice, 47
DeVos, Betsy, 47
diaspora, 38
DPS. *See* Denver Public School District (DPS)
"dropout factories," 52
dropout rates, 5, 11, 24, 30, 67

economic disadvantages, 33
EdLabs, 19
educational equity/inequity, 1–6, 29, 35, 50, 78, 81, 82
educational philosophy, 25
educational systems, xxii, xxiii, 2, 3, 9, 25, 27, 28, 35, 37, 78, 81, 82
education debt, 28
Education Innovation and Research program, 5, 7
education programs, 7, 50
Elementary and Secondary Education Act (ESEA, 1965), 3–4, 7–9, 21
emotional intelligence, 27
employment, 37, 40
English, Fenwick W., 32
equality, concept of, 28–29
ESEA. *See* Elementary and Secondary Education Act (ESEA, 1965)
Every Student Succeeds Act (ESSA, 2015), 5–7, 21
Excellent Educators for All initiative, 8
experiential preparation programs, 73–75

Fair Housing Act (1968), 2
federal education policy, xiii, xix, 7, 12
federal funds, 12, 13, 15, 23, 37
federal government, 4, 11, 21–23
Federal Housing Administration (FHA), xx
federal programs, 6–8, 18, 77
FHA. *See* Federal Housing Administration (FHA)
Flint, Michigan, 34
Freire, Paulo, xx, 25
Fryer, Roland, Jr., 19
funds/funding, 2–4, 8, 9, 12–14, 22, 37, 45, 54, 55, 62, 77
Furman, Gail, 32

Gay, Geneva, 74
Gooden, Mark A., 50
Gorin, Emily, xxi
graduation rates, 3, 5, 11, 21, 24, 44, 47, 57, 58, 76
Grier, Terry, 19

Haddix, Marcelle, 73
Hambrick Hitt, Dallas, 27, 38
Hanna-Attisha, Mona, 34
Harvard Medical School, 42
Harvard's Graduate School of Education, 6–7
Harvard University, 6–7
Hassel, Emily Ayscue, 77
high-poverty schools, 1, 2, 21, 23
high-quality education, 4, 8, 24
HISD. *See* Houston Independent School District (HISD)
Hispanic students, 2, 35
HOLC. *See* Home Owner's Loan Corporation (HOLC)
home mortgages, xx, 2
Home Owner's Loan Corporation (HOLC), 2
Horsford, Sonya Douglass, 32
Houston Independent School District (HISD), 19
Hurley Children's Clinic, 34

i3. *See* Investing in Innovation fund (i3)
IB World, 73
implicit and explicit biases, 46, 51, 69, 79
income inequality, 2
inductive coding, 59
Institute for Multiracial Justice, 29
Institute of Education Services, xxi
Institute of Labor Economics, 31
instructional coaching programs, 50
Investing in Innovation fund (i3), 5, 7, 9

Jim Crow, 31
Johnson, Lyndon, 3, 8
Journal of Negro History, 25
juvenile justice system, 30, 70

K-12, 18; schools, 13, 37, 74; system, 7, 28
Kaiser Permanente, 31
Kendi, Ibram, 40
Kim, Catherine Y., 41
King, Joyce E., 63
Kowal, Julia M., 77
Kunjufu, Jawanza, 67
Kutash, Jeff, xxi

Ladson-Billings, Gloria, 28, 69, 74, 75
Latino students, xix–xxi, 28
Lawrence Public School District, 11, 19
leadership, xxi, 7, 12, 15, 17, 22, 24, 26, 27, 33–35, 38, 52–55, 58, 79. *See also individual leaderships*
lead paint, 33, 80
learning, xix, xxii, 3, 4, 6, 15, 16, 23, 30, 33, 35, 38, 40–42, 44, 68, 69, 71, 82
Learning Policy Institute, 17
Lewis, Chance, 74
Lewis, John, 82
Libassi, C. J., 69
liberation, 25, 80
low-performing schools, xix, xxi, 1, 5, 6, 11, 13, 15, 18, 19, 21–23, 35, 44, 49–50, 53, 75, 76, 81

marginalized students, xxii, 18, 28, 35, 38, 57
Maslow's hierarchy of needs, 44–45
Massachusetts General Hospital, 42
math proficiency, 4–6, 10, 11, 24
mental health, xxiii, 3, 16, 18, 31, 32, 44–46, 54, 77, 80
Meyers, Coby V., 38
microaggressions, 51, 73, 79
Minnesota Department of Education, 48
The Mis-education of the Negro (Woodson), 25
multicultural education, 38–40, 69, 71, 74
multiculturalism, 51

National Center for Education Statistics (NCES), 2, 17, 30, 35
National Dropout Prevention Center, 67
NCES. *See* National Center for Education Statistics (NCES)
NCLB. *See* No Child Left Behind Act (NCLB, 2001)
Newark, New Jersey, 34
New Deal, 2
Nico, Eva, xxi
Nieto, Sonia, 74
No Child Left Behind Act (NCLB, 2001), 4, 7, 8, 17, 21, 22, 77

Obama, Barack, xx
Obama administration, 4, 9, 47
Oglesby, Alicia, 61
oppression, xx, xxii–xxiii, 25, 28, 35, 39, 40, 57, 63–66
optimism, 80

Papa, Rosemary, 32
pedagogy, xxiii, 16, 18, 34, 45, 50, 51, 67, 69, 72
physiological systems, 45
Pitre, Abul A., 30, 31
Post Traumatic Slave Syndrome, 63
poverty, 3, 8, 15, 16, 19, 21, 24, 30, 33, 46, 78

professional development of staff, 49–52, 71–73, 81
Public Impact, 22
public schools, 2–4, 8, 9, 11, 12, 18, 22, 30, 35
punitive discipline practices, 46–49, 79

quality of education, xix, 1, 35
quantitative comparative analysis, 82

race, 28, 34, 39, 46, 52, 55, 61, 65, 73, 78
Race to the Top (RttT) program, 5, 9
racial bias, 70, 73
"Racial Bias in Education: Breaking the Glass Ceiling to Opportunity," 73
racial discrimination, 30–32, 47, 69, 71, 79
racial inequities, 59, 70–71, 74
racial justice/injustices, xxiii, 1, 48–50
racism, 15, 19, 21, 23, 24, 30, 32, 33, 39, 50, 69, 77–80; dysconscious, 63, 79; institutional, 59, 61–64; post-slavery, 31; systemic, xx, 37, 51, 59, 61–64, 82
racist attitudes, 24, 74, 75
radical housing segregation, 2
Rahmatullah, Samira, xxi
reading proficiency, 4–6, 10, 11, 24
redlining, xx, 2, 8
relationship-building, 42–43, 71
"residential security" maps, 2
restart model, 5, 6, 10
restorative justice circle, 41, 71
restorative justice practices, 46–49, 71, 79
Restorative Practices Implementation Guidance, 48
Riley, Jeff, 11
Rockefeller Institute of Government, 10
Rockefeller Institute of Public Policy, 14
Roosevelt, Franklin D., 2
"rounds," concept of, 41
RttT. *See* Race to the Top (RttT) program

Index

scholarship, 58, 69, 80
school administration/administrators, 4, 16–18, 31, 35, 58, 70
school closure model, 5, 6
school culture, xxi, xxii, 24, 27, 44, 55–57, 66, 71, 72, 76; traumatic change in, 17–18
school discipline, 43, 47, 49
school failure, xix, xxii
school improvement, xxi, 8, 9, 15, 18, 23, 43, 44, 53, 81
school improvement grants (SIGs), 5–7, 9–10, 13, 15, 77
school performance, xxi, 3, 15, 37
school struggles, 2, 3, 22, 26, 37, 38, 49
school-to-prison pipeline, 30, 32, 68, 70, 78
School Turnaround Newsletter, 7
science proficiency, 11
SIGs. *See* school improvement grants (SIGs)
slave trade, 39
social emotion, 16, 17, 45, 71, 82
social justice/injustice, xxiii, 32, 50, 51, 56–57, 61, 64, 68, 74, 75
social justice leaders/leadership, xiii, 32, 56, 57, 64, 68, 74
social promotion, 46, 52, 67–68
Southern Education Foundation, 12
Southern Poverty Law Center, 39
staffing, 15, 27
standardized testing, 4, 7, 8, 17, 22, 23, 30, 55, 77
status quo, xxii, 10, 12, 26, 28, 33–35, 63
stereotyping, 46, 74, 75, 79, 81
stress, 44–46, 48, 55, 80
student(s): achievement, xxi, xxii, 5, 10, 28, 37; agency and voices, 40–42; behaviors, 16, 17, 43, 46, 48, 68, 70; challenges, 15, 16, 23; engagement, 18, 48; listening, 43; miseducation, 29, 32, 59, 63, 66–69, 74, 78, 82; performance, 3, 8, 11, 15, 19, 22, 67

suspension and expulsions, xxiii, 3, 16, 24, 29, 30, 37, 43–47, 70–71, 76, 77, 79
sustainability, 10, 13–15, 52

Tallant, Kate, xxi
tax monies, 2, 4, 5, 15
teacher(s): ineffective, 49–50; leaving profession, 17; oppressive mindsets of, 64–66; preparation programs, 75–77; struggles, 45–46; talented, 50
teacher–student relationships, 43, 79–80
teaching, xxii, 8, 17, 27, 39, 42, 47–51, 65
Theoharis, George, 56, 57, 61, 64, 73
transformation model, 5, 10
transformative leaders/leadership, xxii, 11, 26, 35, 56, 58, 61, 74, 76, 82
trauma, 44, 45, 49, 55, 63; childhood, 15–16, 31–33; multigenerational, 63
Trump administration, 23, 47
turnaround efforts, 6–19, 55; failure, 12–18; results of, 9–12
Turnaround for Children, 15, 21
turnaround model, 5, 6, 10
turnaround partnerships, 6–7
turnaround schools, xix, xx, xxiii, 1, 6–8, 11, 12, 16–19, 21, 27, 34, 35, 42, 62, 77, 79, 82; accepting God's calling, 60–61; principals in, xxii, xxiii, 22–24, 37–38, 40, 42, 55–56, 71–72, 77, 78, 81, 82. *See also individual entries*

UCLA Civil Rights Project, 43
United States, xix, xx, 1, 3–5, 9, 18, 34, 69
universities and colleges, xxii, 6, 7, 22, 50, 51, 73, 75
University of Virginia, 7
University of Virginia Partners for Leaders in Education (UVA-PLE), 7
U.S. Department of Education, xx–xxi, 3, 7–10, 13, 15, 30, 43
UVA-PLE. *See* University of Virginia Partners for Leaders in Education (UVA-PLE)

violence, 31, 32, 47, 80
virtual learning, 82

Walmart, 54
"War on Poverty," 3, 8
wealth inequality, 25, 55
white privilege, 28, 61, 64

white students, 2, 28, 29, 35, 67
white supremacy, 25, 28, 29, 32, 61, 78, 80
white teachers, 58, 67, 72, 75
Woodson, Carter G., xxii, 24, 25, 66

Zaff, Jonathan, 47

www.ingramcontent.com/pod-product-compliance
Lightning Source LLC
Chambersburg PA
CBHW030144240426
43672CB00005B/268